A HOUSE DIVIDED

Nevada Senator Bill Raggio and the Fracturing of the GOP

Michael Archer

OTHER BOOKS BY MICHAEL ARCHER

A Man of His Word: The Life and Times of Nevada Senator William J. Raggio

"Mr. Archer has rendered the people of Nevada a fascinating history lesson."
—HARRY REID, United States Senator.

"Archer's thorough research reveals his intellectual honesty and literary balance."
—DAVID HARDY, Judge, Second Judicial District–Nevada.

A Patch of Ground: Khe Sanh Remembered

"An intelligent, courageous, sensitive book about a historic battle in a controversial war."
—KENNETH J CAMPBELL, Professor of International Relations, University of Delaware.

The Long Goodbye: Khe Sanh Revisited

**Foreword magazine INDIES
Book of the Year Award 2016**

"A brutally honest and impassioned work of nonfiction that takes us even deeper inside America's faltering war in Vietnam in early 1968."
—GREGG JONES, Pulitzer Prize finalist, foreign correspondent, and investigative journalist for the *Dallas Morning News*.

✳ ✳ ✳

The Gunpowder Prince: How Marine Captain Mirza Munir Baig Saved Khe Sanh

**2019 Marine Corps Heritage Foundation
Colonel Joseph Alexander Award for Distinguished
Biography**

"A neglected American hero."
—WAYNE KARLIN, award-winning author, editor, Professor Emeritus at the College of Southern Maryland, and Marine combat veteran in Vietnam.

"I recommend this book to military professionals and historians. It is an eminently readable narrative and an eye-opener for those of us who served during that epoch."
—KENT STEEN, Colonel, USMC (retired) and colleague of Captain Mirza Munir Baig during the siege of Khe Sanh.

ACKNOWLEDGMENTS

I wish to thank Pulitzer Prize-winning journalist and author Warren Lerude, longtime University of Nevada Press acquisitions editor Margaret Dalrymple, and especially my wife Becky for sharing their wisdom, encouragement, and advice.

I am deeply grateful to those who provided the cornerstone of this book by sharing their knowledge and invaluable insights, including personal interviews with Joe Brezny, Greg Brower, Richard Bryan, Barbara Buckley, Bob Cashell, Claire Jesse Clift, Robert Dickens, Greg Ferraro, Oscar Goodman, Kenny Guinn, Ira Hansen, Joseph Hardy, Warren Hardy II, Pat Hickey, Mark James, Ben Kieckhefer, Paul Laxalt, Lorne Malkiewich, Dennis Myers, Bill Raggio, Dale Raggio, Jon Ralston, Harry Reid, Bob Rose, Ron Scheberle, Dina Titus, Randolph Townsend, Jerry Watson, and Steve Wynn.

"A house divided against itself cannot stand."

Abraham Lincoln, June 16, 1858
Illinois Republican State Convention

Contents

Introduction

In November 2010, far-right Republican candidate Sharron Angle was on the verge of defeating Democratic U.S. Senate Majority Leader Harry Reid in what was shaping up to be one of the greatest upsets in American political history. However, over two hundred high-profile Nevadans, united under the organizational title "Republicans for Reid," rallied to provide endorsements that proved instrumental in Angle's subsequent defeat, highlighting deep divisions within the Republican Party.

Long-time Republican State Senator Bill Raggio did not join that list; instead, he made a forceful, independent declaration he hoped would open the eyes of his party to the direction it was heading. He explained that he could not endorse Angle because of her "inability or unwillingness to work with others, even within her own party."

Raggio qualified his decision by saying he did not agree with Senator Reid on much of his agenda. Still, as the U.S. Senate Majority Leader, arguably the second most powerful person in the country, Reid would better represent Nevada's interests. As such, Raggio concluded: "I will reluctantly vote for Senator Reid's reelection."

Ultraconservatives in the GOP were furious. The State Senate Republican Caucus quickly drove Raggio from his longtime leadership role. He subsequently resigned his Senate seat. Disowned by many supporters and even lifelong friends, organizations that had once bragged of Raggio's membership now distanced themselves.

Though disappointed, Raggio did not back down, publicly sounding the alarm that extremist factions within the state and national GOP would soon take control and that their refusal to negotiate, in a zealous crusade for ideological purity, would fracture, and consequently weaken, the party to a point where it would no longer be acceptable to a majority of American voters. After decades of perpetuating the belief that the government was an enemy of the American people, these ultraconservatives were willing to shut it down unless others accepted their nonnegotiable social and fiscal agendas.

Raggio had always considered himself a conservative champion of individual rights, limited government, and fiscal responsibility, but in a way that would, as he often said, deliver "lean government, but not a mean government." With this philosophy as his guide, he led the State Senate for decades with a willingness to listen and to consider the opinions of others. Because of this, he gained trust on both sides of the aisle, partisanship was minimal, and legislators generally worked together for the common good. Raggio understood President Ronald Reagan's axiom: "The person who agrees with you 80 percent of the time is a friend and an ally—not a 20 percent traitor."

I came to know Senator Raggio in 2003 when I was assigned as a staff member to his Committee on Finance at the Nevada Legislature. My first book, A *Patch of Ground: Khe Sanh Remembered,* a memoir of my time as a young Marine during the 1968 siege of Khe Sanh in South Vietnam, was released the following year. Because Raggio had been a World War II-era Marine officer, I slipped him a copy in a hallway one Friday afternoon. He read the book that weekend and asked if I would write his biography.

I spent the next several years researching his personal life and career. During that time, I conducted over sixty hours of interviews with Raggio, supplemented by dozens of discussions with his legal and political colleagues—friend and foe. In addition, as a Finance Committee staff member, I observed Senator Raggio daily during biennial legislative sessions over eight years. The result was *A Man of His Word: The Life & Times of Nevada's Senator William J. Raggio,* published in 2011.

Upon his election as Washoe County District Attorney in 1958, Raggio cleaned up widespread corruption in the Reno city government and police department, which generated threats against him and concerns about his family's safety.

His contentious relationship with Nevada's flamboyant brothel owner, Joe Conforte, culminating in a bungled attempt by Conforte to blackmail Raggio, resulted in a conviction for extortion. The lewd content of the trial made it a sensation for its time, covered by national and international news services. As Raggio's fame for being a colorful and effective prosecutor grew, he received several prestigious awards and honors. In 1967, after being named District Attorney of the Year by the National District Attorneys Association, Raggio was elected its president—remarkable recognition for a prosecutor from a small western county.

In those days, Northern Nevada hosted topline entertainment, and Raggio's outgoing personality resulted in long friendships with some of the country's foremost entertainers. Most notable among them was Frank Sinatra. When Nevada gaming officials forced Sinatra to surrender his gaming license as a result of hosting a Chicago mobster at his Cal Neva Lodge at Lake Tahoe, Raggio remained loyal despite being the top cop in the county where that occurred, raising eyebrows and providing fodder for his political foes.

In 1963, when Frank Sinatra Jr. was kidnapped at Lake Tahoe, but outside Raggio's jurisdiction, Bill Raggio was one of the first people Sinatra called on for assistance. In later years, when Sinatra sought a new gaming license in Nevada, Raggio, in private practice as one of the top gaming attorneys in the state, successfully pled the case before the Gaming Control Board, despite evidence that Sinatra had continued to associate with members of organized crime.

As his fame grew, Raggio always kept in mind the people he was elected to serve. *Las Vegas Review-Journal* reporter Jude Wanniski marveled at Raggio's wit and ability "to remember the name of nearly every person he ever met:"

In Reno, it's virtually impossible to sit and talk to him for ten minutes without interruption. In restaurants, the cook comes out of the kitchen to say hello to him. On the street, the truck drivers honk at him, cabbies slow down, yell and wave to him. A hotel porter is sifting cigarette butts out of a wall sandbox; Raggio, walking by, hails him: "Freddie, you find any gold yet?" and the porter turns around and grins.[1]

Just before he and his wife, Dale, left on vacation to Australia in late February 2012, Raggio called me to discuss an upcoming book signing we had scheduled in a few weeks at the Wynn Las Vegas. Three days later, he died from respiratory failure in Sydney. Until the end, despite all it cost him, he never regretted his outspoken resistance to those who had "hijacked" his party or doubted for a moment that his stand was in the best interest of all Nevadans.

What follows is intended to show how this change in Republican Party politics came about and what happened to "old school" conservatives, like Raggio, who predicted political disaster.

1

The Political Waters

ON ELECTION DAY, November 5, 1972, as President Richard M. Nixon trounced South Dakota Senator George McGovern in one of American history's most lopsided presidential elections, forty-five-year-old Bill Raggio claimed a seat in the Nevada State Senate.

Raggio's character was rooted in his parents' and immigrant grandparents' deep respect for American ideals. Growing up through the adversity of the Great Depression and his early passion for scouting taught him the values of self-discipline, thrift, sacrifice, and integrity. After serving as a Marine Corps lieutenant at the end of World War II, Raggio attended the University of Nevada. He subsequently earned a law degree from the University of California and was admitted to the Nevada State Bar in 1952.

He would first vote in 1948, registering as a Republican, later saying:

> I did not heavily identify with either party at that time but believed that the Republican Party represented free enterprise and other ideals I embraced. But my parents and grandparents had been Republicans, so it was not a difficult choice.

Despite his registration preference, in November of that year, he voted for the incumbent Democratic President Harry Truman over Republican challenger Thomas Dewey.

In 1958, Raggio was elected Washoe County District Attorney. In 1968, he ran in the State primary election to become the Republican Party's nominee in the upcoming U.S. Senate race, but was defeated. An editorial in the *Reno Evening Gazette* applauded his effort in making the race so close and speculated that had he entered sooner, he may have had time to make a more significant impression on rural voters in the so-called "Cow Counties."

Yet another, more subtle political dynamic in this race would continue to dog Raggio throughout his political career. In 1959, he participated in burning down a brothel run by Raggio's flamboyant nemesis Joe Conforte in nearby Storey County after the county's district attorney declared it a public nuisance. Though legally a spectator, Raggio would use that colorful event to enhance his public image. To his surprise, it would also become a source of vilification.

While the majority of Nevadans were conservative when it came to the enforcement of the law and punishment of lawbreakers, they also disliked government intrusion into their lives. Nevada's individualistic political culture primarily focused on placing a premium on limiting both governmental and non-governmental community intervention in private activities.[2] Viewed from outside Nevada, this attitude was most apparent in the prerogative by individual county governments to legalize brothel prostitution. Destruction of private property—anyone's personal property—by a government entity was frowned upon. Consequently, many in those rural counties felt Raggio had overstepped the authority of his government position to engage in a personal vendetta against Conforte.

Despite this setback, Raggio found himself increasingly popular with a great many voters who had grown tired of social unrest related to civil rights, the Vietnam War, and President Lyndon Johnson's idealistic public works programs. In a speech as president of the National District Attorneys Association, Raggio spoke on various topics, including recent U.S. Supreme Court rulings, riot control, changes in criminal procedures, and limitations imposed on prosecutors. He promised to change these liberal guidelines "which have inundated this nation in a tragic social experiment within the past several decades."

As his popularity grew, Raggio focused on the Governor's Mansion in Carson City. By early 1970, despite a 3-1 Democratic Party advantage in statewide voter registration, polls showed him holding a wide lead over any other potential challenger. It would have taken a stroke of exceedingly bad luck to prevent Raggio from becoming Nevada's next governor. Yet, such misfortune soon befell him when President Nixon decided to take a personal interest in Bill Raggio's political career.

He was soon under intense pressure from the President, Vice President Spiro Agnew, and other members of the administration, as well as state and national Republican Party leaders, to postpone his dream of being governor and run for the U.S. Senate against incumbent Democrat Howard Cannon. "The governorship of this great State has much appeal to me," he said, "but one does not take lightly a request by his president and vice president."

Loyal to his party, even in the face of a decision he knew to be misguided, Raggio agreed and ran an energetic campaign. Republican Governor Paul Laxalt joined him several times, and distinguished author Robert Laxalt, the governor's brother, assisted with speechwriting. Still, there were problems.

"The Nixon administration did not entirely keep part of the agreement," Raggio said. "My campaign did not get all the funding promised and was left with a deficit."

Raggio and Cannon were close on issues like the Vietnam War, crime, and campus disruption, but Cannon refused to debate the courtroom-eloquent Raggio and did not otherwise offer much of a target. Raggio, on the other hand, was soon saddled with an administration blamed for a faltering national economy and negative political fallout from several unpopular decisions the President made, including the invasion of Cambodia, which resulted in several student protestors being killed by Ohio National Guardsmen at Kent State University—spawning student strikes and civil unrest across the nation.

Nixon eventually cut a deal with Senator Cannon, a decorated World War II veteran who was now an Air Force Reserve major general. In exchange for the president's promise to increase defense spending, Cannon was appointed to the Blue Ribbon Committee investigating the Cambodian invasion. This was essentially a Republican president's mid-election campaign endorsement of Raggio's Democratic opponent.

"We were furious," Raggio later said. "I was sure a deal had been made between the president and Cannon. However, we were in the midst of a campaign, and I could not let it show. You just had to roll with the punches. That's what you did."[3]

Political maneuvering by the White House and not making good on their promise of adequate campaign funding doomed Bill Raggio's bid for the U.S. Senate—barely receiving 40 percent of the votes. "It was the biggest mistake of my political life," Raggio later said. "The White House pulled the rug out from under me after they had persuaded me to run."

He had given up his job to campaign, and now, with a wife and three children to support, he could not wallow in disappointment for long. Within months, he would move to Las Vegas as a partner in a prestigious law firm. But, after sixteen years with the district attorney's office, Raggio longed to return to public service and make a difference. Moving back to Reno, he successfully ran for a seat in the Nevada State Senate, arriving in Carson City ready for business in early 1973 for the 57th Session of the Nevada Legislature.

*****

Democrat Richard Bryan, who would go on to become Nevada's attorney general, governor, and U.S. senator, arrived at the State Senate the same year as Bill Raggio, recalled how many legislators were concerned about Raggio's reputation as "a fire-breathing prosecutor, and a single-issue person, arguing all the time about longer prison sentences, and the like."

"However," Bryan said, "I was pleased to see how seamlessly his transition from prosecutor to legislator was. Even then, he was a man of considerable intellect and immense personal charm and fit into the State Senate like a glove." Raggio later commented, "As a Senator, I had to look at the whole picture, not only the criminal cases but everything else we do."

Despite occasional disagreements, there was little partisan bickering in the Senate, mainly because Democrats were more socially conservative than Republicans, traditionally due to the political power of the rural counties and leadership by what was then termed the "Mormon Mafia."

However, a few years earlier, the Legislature had transformed like at no other time in its history. Despite the Nevada Constitution requiring that apportionment be based on population, the legislature used various plans to determine representation—none proportionate to population. The State Senate was then comprised of one senator from each county, regardless of population disparities, and at least one member in the State Assembly per each county. This method had the effect of over-representing the rural counties at the expense of growing urban areas.[4]

Beginning in 1962, a series of U.S. Supreme Court decisions required states to ensure that both houses of state legislatures be apportioned based on population, then referred to as the "one-man-one-vote" rule.[5] Most Nevada legislators balked at such interference by the federal government and adjourned the 1965 regular legislative session without addressing the matter. To rectify Clark County's considerable underrepresentation in the State Legislature, Democratic Assemblywoman Flora Dungan filed suit against Democratic Governor Grant Sawyer to force the issue.

Nevada's apportionment formula was subsequently ruled unconstitutional. Governor Sawyer called a special legislative session to settle the matter, reminding the legislators that they would almost certainly face judicial reapportionment if they failed to redistrict the State properly.

By the end of the special session, legislative power traditionally held by rural counties had shifted dramatically and permanently to urban areas. Most rural county voters never forgot or forgave what they considered federal government intrusion into State business.

*****

When Raggio arrived at the State Senate, the nation was in cultural and political upheaval due to demands for equal rights, which included equality for women, an unpopular war in Vietnam, and the emerging Watergate scandal. Also, that year, the Legislature would seat its first African-American State Senator, Joseph M. Neal, Jr.

Joe Neal, a thirty-seven-year-old electrical company personnel administrator from North Las Vegas, had spent four years in the Air Force before graduating with a degree in political science from Southern University in 1963. Neal would be part of a sizeable Democratic majority in the Senate but later recalled that the ideological differences between Democrats and Republicans in his first session were so slight, saying: "I was the only true Democrat there."

Raggio, one of only six Republicans, recalled that this first session presented him with one of the most challenging decisions he would ever face as a legislator, implementing *Roe v. Wade*, the U.S. Supreme Court decision legalizing abortion.[6] Feelings ran high on both sides of the issue, but the ruling required the Legislature to act because it conflicted with Nevada's existing law prohibiting abortion.

Raggio took this dilemma to the bishop of the Catholic Diocese in Reno. The cleric told him that, despite the church's doctrine against abortion, he had an obligation to follow the nation's laws, and in doing that, the Church could not fault him. "I could have argued that because I was a Catholic, I was going to refuse to change the law." Raggio later said: "But I saw that as a violation of my oath as a senator because the Supreme Court decision is the law of the land, as much as is an act of Congress. As such, I did vote to change our state law to conform to *Roe v. Wade*."

He was surprised to see how many legislators were reluctant to do that and allowed their personal religious beliefs to influence their votes. After much heated debate, both houses approved the language and entered it into the Nevada Revised Statutes.[7]

18

*****

As Senator Raggio set about learning his new job, he kept one eye on another run at the governorship. Yet, his hope of someday living in the governor's mansion was again dashed when popular incumbent Democrat Mike O'Callaghan phoned him on April 5, 1973, to say he was going to announce his run for reelection the following day. Raggio had hoped O'Callaghan would run for the U.S. Senate, as was rumored, leaving the governorship up for grabs. The governor explained that he had decided against the Senate race because he preferred raising his large family in Nevada.

Raggio remained noncommittal about his next political move until July 17, 1974, nine weeks before the State primary elections, when he announced his bid for the office of lieutenant governor, easily winning the Republican nomination. In Nevada, lieutenant governor and governor candidates do not run on the same ticket but are elected individually. His Democratic opponent in the race would be Bob Rose, who had been Raggio's immediate successor as Washoe County District Attorney.

During the campaign, President Nixon resigned under threat of impeachment. As if that was not enough unnecessary political baggage for Republican candidates to carry, the new president, Gerald R. Ford, immediately pardoned the outgoing president before he was charged with a crime. As a former prosecutor, Nixon's pardon disturbed Raggio's concept of equal justice. However, he believed Ford acted with good conscience in the nation's best interest.

Eerily, it now seemed that Nixon had once again interfered with Raggio's chances of being elected to a statewide office, as he had done in 1970 during his campaign for the U.S. Senate.

Bob Rose, a thirty-four-year-old former State Democratic Party chair, had a large following of young and enthusiastic volunteers. The two ran a cordial but challenging race. In the end, Rose was victorious, garnering 56 percent of the vote.

Veteran Kansas Republican Senator Bob Dole, who barely won reelection that year, saw the national drubbing of Republican candidates as being the result of one thing. "The wreckage of Watergate," he stated, "is spread over the landscape." [8] Rose would later concur with Dole's assessment: "Even the greatest campaigner could not have won that race if they were Republican. Raggio had an awfully tough race. He probably would have beaten me had it not been the Watergate year."

U.S. Senator Harry Reid also reflected on Raggio's statewide office races: "I believe the Republican Party never used him properly in the statewide races—and that was Nevada's loss. Yet Raggio picked himself up after those defeats and did what was best for the State. He became a very successful lawmaker."

Warren Lerude, the editor of the *Reno Evening Gazette,* had often been at odds with District Attorney Raggio over shield laws protecting journalists' confidential sources. At the time, he wrote: "Raggio, returning to the Nevada Senate, may emerge the strongest Republican in the State over the next two years. Considering the present disarray of the party, there will be no one to match him."[9]

2

Fringe Factions

THE UNITED STATES EMERGED from World War II as the world's foremost economic and military power. Still, communism had also strengthened as it swept through Eastern Europe and East Asia. The U.S. was soon engaged in a constant campaign, the Cold War, to curtail the spread of communism by the Soviet Union and the People's Republic of China through indirect, non-confrontational means, though occasionally having things turn into "hot" proxy wars in places like Korea and Vietnam.

The Communist Party USA had claimed membership of 75,000 by the end of the 1930s. Because it was not illegal to be a communist in the United States, arresting one would require a case being made that espionage was occurring on behalf of a hostile nation. By the early 1950s, there were several notable instances in the United States and Great Britain of such spying, which proved to be of particular help to the Soviet Union in catching up with the West in nuclear arms technology.

In April 1948, the House Un-American Activities Committee offered a bill, coauthored by Representative Richard M. Nixon, to proscribe many Communist Party activities without outlawing the party altogether. The bill passed in the House but failed in the Senate.

With information provided privately by FBI Director J. Edgar Hoover, Nixon brought a case against State Department employee Alger Hiss, accused of spying for the Soviet Union in the 1930s. By 1950, the statute of limitations had expired for espionage, so Hiss was tried for perjury based on allegations made by a former member of the U.S. Communist Party. Hiss denied that he had ever been a communist or had spied for the Soviets. The first trial ended in a hung jury, but the second trial brought a conviction, sending Hiss to federal prison. The Hiss case would gain Nixon national public exposure and support within the Republican Party, propelling him to the vice presidency and eventually the White House.

*****

General Dwight D. Eisenhower defeated the more conservative Senator Robert A. Taft in the 1952 Republican presidential primary. Taft was President William Howard Taft's eldest son, who had battled former President Theodore Roosevelt, a progressive, for the soul of the Republican Party. Taft would now lead the conservative wing of the GOP and dominate domestic policies during the Eisenhower administration.

Directing a coalition of conservative Republicans and southern segregationist Democrats, Taft had earlier thwarted Democratic President Harry S. Truman's domestic agenda. Like many conservative Republicans then, Taft felt that New Deal policies had been in place too long—and had lengthened the Depression.

Taft generally opposed any measure he considered "big government" or anti-business and was a vocal critic of liberalism. Not only did he obstruct legislation supported by Truman, but he also passed several significant bills of his own, which was no small achievement considering that Congress required a two-thirds majority to override a presidential veto. One such veto override was the Taft-Hartley Labor Act, which limited the use of strikes and prevented unions from donating directly to political campaigns.

*****

In 1950, shortly after Alger Hiss was convicted, Wisconsin Republican Senator Joseph McCarthy claimed America was in the throes of widespread domestic subversion, at one point insisting there were 205 Communist spies in the State Department.[10] Empowered by a lack of challenges to these claims, McCarthy broadened his attacks.

22

Industries established Black Lists to restrict the employment of those suspected of communist affiliations or sympathy. Many were denied employment based solely on an unsupported accusation. Such restrictions were not an entirely new concept. Three years earlier, President Truman had signed an executive order to screen federal employees for possible association with organizations deemed "totalitarian, fascist, communist, or subversive" or advocating "to alter the form of Government of the United States by unconstitutional means."

As this Red Scare bloomed into hysteria, libraries were pressured to remove "subversive" reading materials. Fear of being slandered by McCarthy drove Americans, who had nothing to hide, into silence. Following the Republican election landslide in 1952, McCarthy turned his investigations toward wildly popular Republican President Eisenhower. Eisenhower, in a thinly veiled reference to McCarthyites within his party, said: "If a political party does not have its foundation in the determination to advance a cause that is right and that is moral, then it is not a political party; it is merely a conspiracy to seize power." [11]

FBI Director J. Edgar Hoover supported and assisted McCarthy, as he had Nixon. A former FBI agent who participated in all of the FBI's major spy cases during the McCarthy period was horrified: "McCarthy lied about his information and figures. He made charges against people that weren't true. McCarthyism harmed the counterintelligence effort against the Soviet threat because of the revulsion it caused, and all along, Hoover was helping him."[12]

Influential Americans were still unwilling to publicly challenge McCarthy and his methods until March 1954, when one of the nation's most trusted broadcast journalists, Edward R. Murrow, presented a television piece consisting mainly of clips of McCarthy haranguing various witnesses before his committee and accusing the Democratic Party of "twenty years of treason," and the American Civil Liberties Union of being a front for the Communist Party.

Murrow reminded Americans that they should not confuse "dissent with disloyalty" and that "accusation is not proof." He told his audience that this was no time for those opposed to

Senator McCarthy's methods to keep silent and that McCarthy had given considerable comfort to our enemies, saying, "We cannot defend freedom abroad by deserting it at home," and by failing to stand up against such tactics, "we cannot escape responsibility for the result."[13]

Murrow's words inspired a nationwide opinion backlash against McCarthy. To counter the negative publicity, McCarthy charged that Murrow conspired with the "Russian espionage and propaganda organization,"[14] further diminishing McCarthy's credibility. On December 2, 1954, the U.S. Senate voted to "condemn" McCarthy by a vote of 67 to 22. The Democrats were unanimous; Republicans split evenly.

Yet McCarthy retained a zealous support base, with about one-third of the public backing his anti-communist campaign. The Senate vote moved McCarthyism out of Washington D.C. rather than ending it. Now venerated as victimized by a corrupt and self-interested Washington establishment, the McCarthy myth fueled the "politics of grievance" in the modern far-right conservative movement.

Four years later, candy mogul Robert Welch, Jr. founded the John Birch Society, which had as its fundamental doctrine a belief that the greatest enemy of America was its government. The federal government, Welch contended, was inherently corrupt and the primary threat to peace in the world. Private institutions, small local governments, and rugged individualism were the only solutions. Adherents abhorred President Roosevelt for conceding too much to Stalin at the war's end. They considered him a socialist, if not a communist sympathizer, whose New Deal programs had brought about the modern welfare state.

President Eisenhower's efforts in bringing down McCarthy, his peace treaty with communists ending the Korean conflict, and the president's implementation of school integration in the South convinced Welch that Eisenhower was either a communist or communist dupe:

> Both the U.S. and Soviet governments are controlled by the same furtive conspiratorial cabal of internationalists, greedy bankers, and corrupt

politicians. If left unexposed, the traitors inside the U.S. government would betray the country's sovereignty to the United Nations for a collectivist New World Order managed by a 'one-world socialist government.[15]

Soon, even champions of Wall Street had had enough. In 1962, William F. Buckley Jr., editor of the influential conservative magazine *National Review*, denounced Welch and the John Birch Society as "far removed from common sense" and urged the GOP to purge itself of Welch's influence. Buckley was beginning to worry that with the John Birch Society proliferating, "the right-wing upsurge in the country would take an ugly, even Fascist turn."[16]

Radical right-wing paramilitary organizations were springing up. Typical was The Minutemen, a militant, nativist group that feared an imminent communist takeover of the United States. Organized into small cells and stockpiling weapons for an anticipated counter-revolution, their plans included violently suppressing any person or organization they deemed un-American.

The baseless and defamatory charges against President Eisenhower by Welch prompted numerous other conservative Republicans, including Bill Raggio, Paul Laxalt, and nationally prominent Arizona Senator Barry Goldwater, to renounce the group.

Some historians have argued that the ideology of the John Birch Society and other radical-right organizations suggests a readiness to jettison constitutional processes and to suspend liberties, consciously emulating Communist cell-style methods through 'front' groups and waging ideological war along similar lines—the end justifying the means. Before Barry Goldwater renounced the organization, he was a vocal supporter of this method, once saying: "I would suggest that we analyze and copy the strategy of the enemy; theirs has worked and ours has not."[17]

*****

San Francisco hosted the Republican National Convention in July 1964 to nominate a candidate to challenge President Lyndon Johnson. Johnson had yet to win a presidential election, having assumed the office upon the assassination of President Kennedy just eight months earlier. Lieutenant Governor Paul Laxalt and Washoe County District Attorney Bill Raggio attended the raucous, tension-filled affair. Conservative supporters of Senator Barry Goldwater openly clashed with liberal and moderate backers of New York Governor Nelson Rockefeller. When Rockefeller attempted to deliver a speech, far-right delegates on the convention floor booed and loudly denounced him as a member of "the eastern liberal establishment." Goldwater was easily nominated.

In his acceptance speech, Goldwater declared that communism was the "principal disturber of the peace in the world today" and then delivered the phrase for which the world would most remember him: "I would remind you that extremism in the defense of liberty is no vice. And let me remind you also that moderation in the pursuit of justice is no virtue."[18] With those words, he lost the moderates and liberals within his party—effectively ending his chances of being elected. Goldwater's rhetoric frightened most Americans, who returned President Johnson in an electoral landslide.

While the Laxalt-led Nevada delegation cast the State's six delegate votes for Goldwater at the convention as a gesture of unity, earlier that year at the Nevada State Republican convention, Laxalt and Raggio worked successfully to pass a hotly contested resolution, the effect of which was to muscle out rightist splinter groups, like the Birchers, and mediate disputes between the far-right and more centrist factions.[19]

What Raggio saw in San Francisco disturbed him. Moderates, who felt the platform should concentrate on policies that would stimulate economic growth, had been pushed aside by a right-wing element with ideological ties to McCarthyism and fueled by the conspiracy-driven John Birch Society. Though politically conservative, Raggio was fact-driven and felt such factions within the party were dangerously paranoid.

But what Laxalt and Raggio wished the Republican Party to be was not accepted by all. Goldwater Republicans believed themselves to be the party's rank-and-file, and after Taft died in 1953, they became increasingly dissatisfied that the party was ignoring their needs. By the end of that decade, the GOP would begin a swing back to the right—with a vengeance.

*****

Anti-government Communist conspiracy theories were not the only thing threatening to change the philosophy of the Republican Party during the early 1960s. After President Johnson signed the Civil Rights Act in 1964, White segregationist southern Democrats, still chafing after several generations of having Black equality forced upon them by Republicans during post-Civil War Reconstruction, now flocked to the party of Lincoln. After signing the historic legislation, Johnson told an aide: "I think we just delivered the South to the Republican Party for a long time to come."[20]

Most Southerners had been dissatisfied with the Democratic Party for some time. Throughout the Franklin Roosevelt presidency, First Lady Eleanor was a vocal champion of racial equality. At the party's national convention in 1948, President Harry Truman added a civil rights plank to the platform, resulting in the racial integration of the armed forces. In opposition, the States' Right Party, or Dixiecrats, nominated South Carolina Democratic Governor Strom Thurmond as their candidate during a rump convention held in Birmingham, Alabama.

The U.S. Supreme Court's 1954 unanimous ruling in the case of *Brown v. Board of Education* brought the issue of school desegregation to national attention. Southern Democratic leaders initiated a campaign of resistance. Institutionalized violence against Blacks in the South increased. In Little Rock, Arkansas, President Eisenhower ordered U.S. Army paratroopers to protect nine Black teenagers integrating into a public school, the first time since Reconstruction federal troops were deployed in the South to settle civil rights issues, accelerating the frequency of physical assaults and murders against civil rights activists, and the bombings of Black churches and schools by Whites.

By 1957, only about 20 percent of black Americans were registered to vote.[21] Despite being the majority population in numerous counties and congressional districts in the South, most Blacks had been effectively disfranchised by Southern Democrats using discriminatory voter registration rules and laws such as literacy tests and poll taxes. While these states had the right to establish rules for voter registration concerning state and local elections, the U.S. government had an oversight role in ensuring that citizens could exercise the Constitutional right to vote for federal officers, including members of Congress and the president.[22] Federal officials seeking to exercise this oversight validated in the minds of many white Southerners that the U.S. government was their enemy.

Resistance by Whites to racial equality promised by the Civil Rights Act of 1964 also fueled the anger and frustration felt by many Blacks. The Civil Rights movement then was best known for Gandhi-inspired, nonviolent protests associated with Dr. Martin Luther King Jr. However, the Student Nonviolent Coordinating Committee (SNCC), initially committed to the registration and mobilization of black voters in the deep South, and student sit-ins at segregated lunch counters, splintered in the mid-1960s, mainly as a reaction to growing violence by Whites against them in the South. While most were eventually absorbed into the Southern Christian Leadership Conference, Democratic Party politics, or work in federally-funded, anti-poverty programs, many could no longer abide by non-violent methods and made a short-lived attempt to merge with the militant Black Panther Party.

On another front, activist Malcolm X, who served for a dozen years as the public face of the Nation of Islam, criticized the mainstream civil rights movement for its emphasis on nonviolence and racial integration. The Nation advocated for Black empowerment, the separation of Black and White Americans, and urged fellow Black Americans to protect themselves against White aggression "by any means necessary."[23] The first of many years of urban riots in the United States exploded in Watts, California, during the summer of 1965, triggered by alleged police brutality while arresting a young black man suspected of drunk driving. Other riots would follow in almost every major city in the country, especially following the assassination of Dr. King in April 1968.

Often touched off by an act or rumor of police brutality, rioters targeted local businesses with looting, vandalism, and arson, a departure from past race riots where attacks were usually against other groups. From 1964 to 1971, there were more than 750 riots, killing 228 people and injuring 12,741 others. After more than 15,000 separate incidents of arson, many predominately Black urban neighborhoods were in ruins.[24] In 1969, White fear, accompanied by an American public tired of the Vietnam War, catapulted Republican Richard M. Nixon into the presidency with his pugnacious vice-presidential pick, Spiro T. Agnew.

Throughout the twentieth century, working-class voters had been an essential component of the Democratic base. But, beginning in the 1970s, once-powerful labor unions shrunk in membership as manufacturing moved abroad. The loss of these jobs, racial integration, and school busing outside the South, coupled with a patriotic defense of the Nixon Administration stepping up attacks against North Vietnamese forces in Cambodia, pushed conservative blue-collar workers into the Republican camp.

On May 8, 1970, about four hundred New York City "Hard Hat" construction workers, joined by about eight hundred office workers, violently broke up a student demonstration protesting the recent killing of antiwar protesters by Ohio National Guardsmen at Kent State University. For one observer, the riot captured "when FDR's everyman first turned against the liberalism that once had championed him," and President Nixon "moved the Republican Party from blue bloods to blue collars." [25]

*****

Many of those fleeing to the Republican side were reacting to the left-wing radicalization of the Democratic Party. During the 1960s, socialist organizations gained influence and political credibility through their grassroots contributions to the civil rights movement, improving labor conditions and implementing anti-poverty and healthcare programs during the Johnson Administration's socially liberal "Great Society."

By 1965, the socialist League for Industrial Democracy and The Students for a Democratic Society (SDS) clashed over ideology when the SDS wanted a more hardline approach to social change. The most extreme was a vote to remove from its constitution a clause that had excluded advocates of, or apologists for, totalitarianism, which included communists.[26]

Membership in the SDS had risen to over 25,000, with chapters springing up on scores of college campuses. They viewed the Vietnam War as misguided foreign policy and the consequence of a social system based primarily on profiting the nation's ruling elite. With a growing militancy modeled after the recent "Black Power" radicalization of the civil rights movement, student activists nationwide grew increasingly confrontational. Tactics included the occupation of university and college administration buildings and organized resistance to the military draft.

At their national convention in 1968, most SDS members voiced a distinctly anarchist platform—destroy the current political system in America but with nothing specific to replace it. However, by their convention in 1969, having now allowed disciplined Marxist cadre into the organization, most delegates backed an ideology of replacing the current U.S. government with a socialist system modeled on variations of existing communist states. Chris Harman, British journalist and long-time member of the Socialist Workers Party, later wrote of that convention: "Everyone thought himself or herself a Marxist; most were Maoists; and while some found it hard to swallow, the bulk of the leadership openly identified with Stalin."[27]

Overly radicalized, the SDS began to collapse later that year, and several leftist domestic terror groups soon appeared, including the highly publicized Symbionese Liberation Army, utilizing bank robberies, kidnapping, and murder, among other violent acts, to achieve their goal of revolution. Others included the New World

Liberation Front and the communist May 19th organization, named for Ho Chi Minh and Malcolm X's common birthdate.

Atop the FBI's Most Wanted List were members of the Weather Underground, also inspired by communist revolutionary ideologies and embracing violence and crime to advance their aim, "the destruction of U.S. imperialism and form a classless communist world."[28] The Weathermen would eventually take part in jailbreaks and instigate riots. Targets of their bombing campaign included the U.S. Capitol, the Pentagon, the California Attorney General's office, and a New York City police station. In 1981, Weathermen members murdered two police officers and a Brinks driver during a bungled armored car robbery. But, with the end of the Cold War and Communist Party rule in the Soviet Union, attacks by these left-wing terrorist groups ceased.

After the American withdrawal from Vietnam in 1973, the antiwar movement disappeared. The idealism sparked by the significant social changes in the 1960s found new causes for the former antiwar activists, inspiring organized efforts to gain equality and benefit for other groups: women, Native Americans, gays and lesbians, migrant workers, and the elderly. Still, other idealists focused on promoting ecological consciousness, issues deemed too progressive in the eyes of many conservative-minded voters.

By the end of the 1970s, the two major political parties had reconstituted themselves. Mainstream bases shifted, with Southern states becoming more consistently Republican in presidential politics and Northeastern states becoming more dependably Democratic.

3

Ideological Sorting

THE NOVEMBER 1980 ELECTION of Ronald Reagan over incumbent President Jimmy Carter was one of the most notable landslide victories in U.S. political history. Reagan had been a well-known film and television actor for decades and was more recently Governor of California.

His political career had taken off in October 1964 during a nationally televised endorsement of then-Republican presidential candidate Barry Goldwater. Governor Reagan delivered a powerful speech laying out an ideology distrustful of the government:

> You and I are told we must choose between a left or right, but I suggest there is no such thing as a left or right. There is only an up or down. Up to man's age-old dream–the maximum of individual freedom consistent with law and order–or down to the ant heap of totalitarianism.[29]

The speech set in motion a new conservative movement in American politics, displacing GOP liberals and moderates, with Reagan as its leader going forward.

Reagan regularly departed from fiscal conservatism as governor by approving tax increases that raised rates. In addition, he approved increased sales taxes and taxes on banks, corporate profits, and inheritances. However, he appeased most of his conservative critics of those taxes with his hawkish support of the Vietnam War and the no-nonsense treatment of anti-war protests on University of

California campuses—which were becoming increasingly violent and deadly—twice calling the National Guard to restore order. His continued criticism of "big government" and calls for welfare reform, even criticizing the Family Assistance Plan recently introduced by President Nixon, was music to their ears.

Reagan tapped into religious voters and traditional Democratic working-class voters in the northern states, who called themselves "Reagan Democrats." Not only were voters shifting to the Republican side, but many incumbent public officeholders were also.

Men were now turning out in more significant numbers to vote. He told Vietnam-era veterans and their families that, despite the outcome of the war and the politically driven equivocation about how the military should conduct it, they had answered the call and gone to war with "noble intentions." After years of these veterans feeling disrespected and unappreciated by the general public, this message resonated. He had redeemed them, and they would not forget it, voting Republican for decades after that.

*****

The 1980 election in Nevada demonstrated this growing conservatism. In statewide races, Republicans did well. Senator Paul Laxalt had an easy race for reelection. Already famous throughout Nevada, his well-publicized friendship with Reagan, forged when they were governors of adjoining states, carried him to victory in every county.

Yet, in the Legislature, Democrats held the same majorities as in the previous year: a fifteen-to-five margin in the Senate and a twenty-six-to-fourteen margin in the Assembly. In his second State of the State Address, Republican Governor Robert List called for austerity because the national economic recession had adversely affected Nevada's gaming industry.

Revenues from sales tax and gaming declined during an economic recession when Nevadans most needed state services. The state was broken, and though Nevada voters had directly contributed to this problem in their overwhelming desire to shift the revenue burden

33

away from property and income taxes, they blamed the governor. Yet, in 1982, while Governor List lost to Democratic challenger Richard Bryan, Republicans took more statewide offices than they had held since 1930.

At this moment in Nevada's political history, Bill Raggio made a deft maneuver that would cement his role as the most potent, non-statewide elected official for years to come. List's defeat left a leadership vacuum within the party, and Raggio was the obvious choice to fill that void. Instead, he made a calculated decision never to seek statewide office again, gaining the trust of those who might otherwise have felt him a challenger in the future.

Democratic Lieutenant Governor Bob Cashell would move to the Republican Party after being personally invited to do so by President Reagan during a White House visit. Like several others in the Assembly and Senate, Cashell would find that their conservative values and pro-business philosophy made them feel unwelcome due to the increasingly liberal social agenda championed by the Democratic Party. Cashell recalled how Governor O'Callaghan called to chastise him for his defection:

> Governor O'Callaghan knew that he would not have been elected governor without moderate Republicans, and U.S. Senator Paul Laxalt would not have been elected without the votes of moderate Democrats. This is an important element of Nevada politics, which fringe factions often ignore.

*****

The 1984 election had been another good one for the Republican Party, and Nevada voted overwhelmingly for the reelection of President Reagan. Though still outnumbered by Democrats in voter registration, Nevada Republican candidates gained significant victories in essential areas and regained a Republican majority in the Assembly for the first time since 1971.

The Nevada Republican Party enjoyed increased prestige from the close personal relationship between President Reagan and U.S.

Senator Paul Laxalt. Several high-level government appointments went to Nevadans, including the appointment of attorney Frank Fahrenkopf as Chair of the Republican National Committee. Fahrenkopf, a 1962 graduate of the University of Nevada, would serve as Chair for six of President Reagan's eight years in the White House, leading the party through two successful presidential campaigns in 1984 and 1988. Stepping down in 1989, he would remain influential and respected in shaping national policy.

Former Republican State Senator Randolph Townsend, who as an incumbent crossed over from the Democrats after President Reagan's first election, believed 1984 was the year American politics changed forever: "In that year, the whole culture changed because of Newt Gingrich," Townsend said in a 2022 interview:

> Until then, legislators would negotiate in a way that allowed everyone to take something home to their constituents. No matter how hardball the negotiations became, no one took it personally. But with Gingrich, it was all about personal attacks and name-calling.

Representative Newt Gingrich of Georgia was first elected in 1978 when the Republican Party was in shambles after Watergate. Gingrich was impatient to see his party rebuilt and felt that as long as Republicans kept compromising with Democrats, the GOP would never reclaim the majority. As such, he set about to destroy traditional bipartisan coalitions that were essential in keeping the process moving forward "and then seize on the resulting dysfunction to wage a populist crusade against the institution of Congress itself… making people so disgusted by Washington they would throw everybody who was in, out." [30]

In 1984, Gingrich recruited a cadre of a dozen similarly minded young members of Congress into the Conservative Opportunity Society, who chose moments when the press was watching to demonstrate their hostility and break with the traditional etiquette of the institution. Gingrich challenged his party's leadership through GOPAC, recruiting and training candidates sympathetic to his crusade. As a former college history professor, Gingrich would later explain his style: "The news media loves fights… When you give them confrontations, you get attention; when you get attention, you can educate."

They had little interest in legislating, instead choosing to make the House of Representatives an arena for conflict and drama. Gingrich quickly recognized the potential power of recently installed C-SPSAN television cameras and began delivering unrestrained tirades against Democrats to an empty chamber, knowing his remarks would reach millions of Americans.

His rhetoric grew bolder with each passing day, accusing Democrats of being corrupt, un-American, pro-communist, and out to destroy the United States,[31] epithets frequently used by the John Birch Society. Eventually, these rants were aimed at moderates in his party, including widely respected U.S. Senator Bob Dole, whom Gingrich called "the tax collector for the welfare state."[32]

Since the end of World War II, lawmakers had adhered to a specific set of norms and traditions, as described by congressional scholar Thomas Mann: "They believed in genuine deliberation and compromise, and they had institutional loyalty." In recent years, however, tectonic shifts in American politics—particularly around race and civil rights issues—had triggered an ideological sorting between the two parties. Liberal Republicans and conservative Democrats were beginning to vanish, and with them, the cross-party partnerships that had fostered cooperation.

Mann observed that it gradually went from legislating to the weaponization of legislating, to the permanent campaign, to the endless war. "It's like he [Gingrich] took a wrecking ball to the most powerful and influential legislature in the world."[33] This hastened political polarization in the country and increased partisan prejudice.[34]

Many believe 1984 was also the advent of post-truth politics, where appeals to emotion and personal belief were more influential in shaping public opinion than verifiable facts. This coincided with the first year The Rush Limbaugh Show was aired on radio. Some found these events strangely paralleled author George Orwell's classic *1984*, which centers mainly around the effectiveness of repeated propaganda and false information.

*****

Fractures in the Republican Party were not merely between moderates and right-wing radicals. Representative Ron Paul, a Republican congressman from Texas, had supported Ronald Reagan for president early in the late 1970s. But, after Reagan's election in 1980, Paul quickly became disillusioned with the administration's policies. He resigned from the House of Representatives in 1984 and abandoned the Republican Party, saying:

> Ronald Reagan and the Republican Party have given us skyrocketing deficits and, astoundingly, a doubled national debt. How is it that the party of balanced budgets, with control of the White House and Senate, accumulated red ink greater than all previous administrations put together?[35]

Paul's message was that the United States government is an enemy of its citizens and neither major political party can be trusted.

Later, as the Libertarian Party presidential candidate in 1988, Paul called Reagan "a dramatic failure," adding that "the Republicans are on their way out as a major party." "Reagan's record is disgraceful," Paul said. "He starts wars, breaks the law, supplies terrorists with guns made at taxpayers' expense, and lies about it to the American people." [36]

The adversarial style that Gingrich was bringing to the U.S. Congress and Ron Paul to the national political debate also infected the cultures of state governments. The 1985 Nevada legislative session would become one of the most bitterly fought and politicized in the State's history.

No better example of this hostility was when, in the closing days of the session, the Republicans in the Assembly voted retroactive bonuses to employees and university personnel but refused them to public school teachers. The press labeled this action as punishing

37

teachers for not endorsing Republican candidates in the 1984 election. The decision to refuse bonus payments to teachers appeared even more "mean-spirited" after the Assembly followed up by voting elected officials a 19 percent increase in salary.

Senator Raggio went against the wishes of his fellow Republicans in the Assembly, leading Senate Republicans to repudiate the action. Indeed, he was annoyed with the Teacher's Association, which had suddenly become solidly partisan, endorsing only Democratic candidates. Raggio had always supported teachers, and they had helped him in return. The Washoe County Teachers Union president admitted to him in 1984 that the National Education Association had pressured them not to endorse Republican candidates, regardless of how friendly their record was toward education. Putting his personal feelings aside, Raggio sponsored a bill to restore bonus pay to teachers. The measure passed in both houses.

In 1987, Republicans finally gained a majority in the State Senate, and Raggio, after fourteen years in the minority party, became Majority Floor Leader and Chair of the Finance Committee. Over those years, he had learned that if he wanted to get anything done, he would have to work with Democrats and interest groups he had previously mistrusted. "Once he started dealing with Democrats as actual people, instead of as vague others," journalist Dennis Meyers wrote, "something he rarely had to do as a prosecutor, politics for him became easier and more congenial."[37]

As another political observer wrote, Raggio set the tenor for the Senate with his professional appearance and style:

> Raggio sought to create a more professional milieu and knew the significance of finding common ground for compromise rather than seeking confrontation. He discovered that most men and women in the Legislature responded better to calm reasoning and humor than to bombast and bluster. His was a leadership that exercised power with finesse.[38]

Raggio benefited from building a good working relationship with his Democratic counterpart in the State Assembly, Speaker Joe Dini from rural Yerington. Though they shared the same heritage, Raggio and Dini were nothing alike. Where Raggio was charming and manifestly clever, Dini was low-key and contemplative, an incarnation of the quiet Westerner who said little, but when he did, everyone listened. Of Raggio, Dini once said, "There is not a lot of politicking going on; we can sit down and work out our problems, get past the issues, play it straight up."

Lorne Malkiewich, longtime Director of the Legislative Counsel Bureau, said, "Dini and Raggio loved the game, but they loved Nevada more, and that was always the bond that brought them together at the end of the session to reach the final agreements." Raggio credited Dini, who had been in the Legislature six years longer, with teaching him how that "game" was played. "I put my name on thirty bills one year," Raggio said, "and Joe held every one of them" to leverage for his aims.

Raggio quickly mastered using parts of proposed legislation by fellow legislators—often those in the other house or party—to artfully quilt together what he wanted, once telling a reporter, "I have nothing with my fingerprints on it." Most importantly, he found that he could better influence policy decisions through the budget process.

As Raggio's enigmatic style evolved, it initially unsettled his fellow legislators. Barbara Buckley would later recall that, as the new Democratic Assembly Speaker in 2007, she experienced "a bit of a learning curve" in dealing with Senator Raggio. "He always intimidated me a little bit before I got to know him," Buckley recalled:

> One thing I learned early on is that he has the ability to put someone at ease very quickly because he can be very charming and very funny. In time, I also learned his negotiating style, which, simply put, is that he will not be moved before he is ready to move. Over the years, Senator Raggio has learned that he can get a lot more if he holds out.

Republican Senator Warren Hardy would later say:

Raggio almost always got everything he wanted. Even after that, he never disclosed exactly what he wanted, even in informal personal conversations, because he knew he would need that dynamic in the following sessions. No one ever knew what his priorities were.

Hardy added that Raggio had a distinct advantage over others because "he slept in his own bed." Most legislators lived either in Clark County or at some distance in the rural counties. They had businesses to run and families to rejoin. Raggio knew that the Legislature would have to do something eventually and that most members would be worn down by the 120-day session and reluctant to risk staying around for as many special sessions as needed.

Not all his legislative colleagues admired Raggio's process. Democratic Senator Joe Neal described Raggio's style as "Very slick, but too cunning. I would say he is average as a leader. He may not pressure others, but they are afraid to oppose him."

4

Fair Share and Sectionalism

DEMOCRAT DINA TITUS, a political science professor at the University of Nevada, Las Vegas, was among the new faces in the Nevada Senate for the 1989 session. Her style was confrontational and feminist, and, like Neal, she directed a good deal of public abuse at Raggio, believing that, as an older white male, he was part of the problem. The level of civility was about to undergo a drastic change.

Because he had always worked so closely with Democratic Senator Jim Gibson, who had died the previous year, Raggio anticipated that he and Titus would have the same rapport. Senator Randolph Townsend later said that, despite her best efforts, Titus was never comfortable negotiating directly with Raggio:

> Senator Titus did a marvelous job as a minority leader. I do not know why she could not sit down and talk to Bill. It may have been because her feminist values were offended by his chivalrous style. I think Bill truly wanted to be able to deal with her directly, but it just never happened.

Years later, Congresswoman Titus reflected upon her years in the Nevada Senate. She said partisanship had evolved from regional differences, the south against the north, urban Las Vegas against the "cow counties," in which she included Washoe. However, as Reno grew and began to experience the same urban problems as Las Vegas, their differences lessened.

Political parties in Nevada, she added, also reflected the growing mood of national partisanship. More women were elected, and redistricting altered the equation, giving the South more seats in the Legislature. "This changed the way we did a lot of our business," Titus said:

> The old ways of drinking, fighting, and negotiating in Jack's Bar across the street no longer worked. I think in the early years, the differences Bill and I experienced were generational. He is kind of old school, Italian and northern, whereas I was Southern, new generation, and a woman.

Republican Senator Ann O'Connell of Clark County, who had arrived four years before Titus, often found Raggio's "old school" ways overly paternalistic:

> He's two personalities to work with, just very, very thoughtful, very, very concerned about his group—but 'Father Knows Best' is his style of operating. I kept reminding him that every one of us was voted in the same way to get to the Legislature, and so I felt that my opinion was as important as his opinion. He never quite bought that. I don't know why.

By the election of 1990, the central political dynamic in Nevada had moved from inter-party to inter-sectional, starting with a flurry of Republican-funded television ads warning that a Democrat-controlled State Senate would mean higher taxes for Washoe County, a reference to money Clark County legislators claimed was owed their constituents as the result of a recently discovered accounting error made by the Washoe County Assessor's Office.

State Democratic Party Chair Tick Segerblom called for Raggio's resignation. "As the second most powerful politician in Nevada," Segerblom said, "he should use his position to promote all regions of Nevada, not just his personal power base. It is unconscionable for him to use his leadership position to deny any part of the State its fair share of State tax revenues." [39]

Senator Neal publicly scolded southern Nevada Republican legislators, asking, "Are they going to be the party of the north, as their leader Bill Raggio dictates? Or are they going to stand up for the people of southern Nevada?"

Unbeknownst to most, much of the funding for those Republican campaign ads came from southern Nevada. Las Vegas-based political journalist Jon Ralston warned readers not to be misled by the belief that most southern Nevadans wanted Raggio removed from office. "Nothing could be further from the truth," Ralston wrote. "Most politically savvy gaming industry executives, and the business community, remain in Republican hands as a conservative foil to any more liberal measures they view as detrimental to their bottom lines."

Ralston quoted one southern Nevada business leader as saying, "The cost of my gaining stability may be more money going to Washoe County and UNR [University of Nevada-Reno] in northern Nevada." [40]

Despite a coffer full of campaign funds from the South, Raggio could not save the Senate majority. On November 7, 1990, voters turned out in large numbers across Nevada. Democrats not only retained their majority in the Assembly but also captured the Senate by an eleven-to-ten margin.

*****

Raggio was disappointed by the results of the 1990 election that now put him back in the minority—and no longer chair of the powerful Committee on Finance. He could see the obstacles ahead, and it was not just the issue of a fair share. With twelve of the twenty-one State Senators now from Clark County (four in the Republican caucus), his continuing leadership role was uncertain. In addition, redistricting during this session would undoubtedly move even more legislative seats to the south and, given the lopsided voter registration favoring Democrats in Clark County, made a return to majority status by Republicans seem improbable. Raggio was stoical, saying, "I was

43

in the minority for fourteen years, so I know how to function in both majority and minority positions."

The Republican caucus again chose him as its leader. Some made the usual rumblings about the need for southern Nevada leadership, but most understood it would take all his experience, intellect, and political skills to navigate the coming session's increasingly hostile political landscape. Yet, not even a veteran like Raggio could then envision what pundit Jon Ralston later called "some of the most[41] mean-spirited, ugly, and unseemly behavior in legislative annals."

A hint of the approaching discord occurred a month before the 1990 election when Senate Democrats removed Senator Neal from his position as minority floor leader, leaving Neal bitter for the remainder of his career. Senator Jack Vergiels, who led the coup, claimed that this action was because Neal was alienating potential campaign contributors.

Vergiels, now the new majority leader, was a fifty-four-year-old professor at the University of Nevada, Las Vegas. Though not as gifted an orator as his predecessor, Raggio, and weaker on policy issues, Vergiels was a shrewd political operative whose single goal was to get Democrats elected—and reelected.

Now facing a $300 million State budget deficit, the passage of a controversial business activity tax, the bitter "fair share" issue, and thorny redistricting decisions, the level of partisanship in both houses became so intense that it seemed to preclude any chance at compromise. The process slowly ground to a halt. Minority Floor Leader Raggio used the leadership vacuum to his advantage, halting progress on the tax package by focusing on the provocative "fair share" issue. On June 27, he amended the proposed fair share bill to reduce the loss to Washoe County significantly.

Democratic Senator Dina Titus angrily derided the proposal during a floor debate, calling Washoe County a "sponge" that has been soaking up taxes Clark and other counties raised. Referring obliquely to Raggio, Titus said the South represented 70 percent of the state: "I never cease to be amazed by the audacity of Washoe County."

Raggio responded angrily, saying that "while the South may represent 70 percent of the State, it is responsible for 90 percent of the problems," warning that such rhetoric risked greater divisiveness. Not surprisingly, his amendment was roundly defeated.

Washoe County citizens were more angered by having to reimburse Clark County than by anything the Legislature had done in memory. They argued that the act was purely punitive, deliberately designed by Clark County lawmakers to penalize Washoe taxpayers for an error that was not their fault.

Despite their victory, many southern Nevada legislators remained disgruntled when they later realized that Senator Raggio anticipated this legislative battle during the previous session and quietly cut the amount of sales taxes Clark County Democrats sought to recover from Washoe County from $13 million to $6.6 million.

An editorial in the *Reno Evening Gazette* praised him for his accomplishments against the angry and suspicious majority from the south. "Raggio," it said, "has become the closest thing to a folk hero that Washoe has had in a long time." [42] But, in doing so, it forever villainized him for many in the southern part of the State.

Arguably, Raggio's most brilliant political move during the 1991 session was seeing Assemblywoman Patricia Little's defection from the Democratic caucus as an opportunity to rally lethargic Assembly Republicans into derailing the Democrats' districting legislation. The Assemblywoman had objected to her party's reapportionment plan, and Raggio, with the assistance of Senator Ann O'Connell, used her alienation to design a strategy that led to an eventual agreement on redistricting more favorable to Republicans.

On June 30, 1991, just hours before the end of the fiscal year, the Legislature approved a $2.2 billion budget. Although aided by improved data collection methods and state-of-the-art computer mapping techniques, the 1991 redistricting process produced partisan and regional bickering, turning it into the most challenging and controversial reapportionment task in the State's history. The Legislature chose to retain the same number of seats, twenty-one in the Senate and forty-two in the Assembly. Washoe County lost one Senate and two Assembly seats to Clark.

*****

The narrow election of Mark James to the State Senate in 1992 gave Republicans the majority they had been hoping to regain. Senator Raggio's profound effect as majority leader on Nevadans' lives over the next fourteen years came about by the slimmest of margins—just thirty-two votes.

On January 18, 1993, the 67th Nevada Legislature convened. Raggio's Senate majority hung by the thinnest of threads. He realized that to maintain it, he would have to diminish confrontation between parties, but just as importantly—within his own. He noted that the machinery of the Republican Party could no longer be relied upon to help recruit candidates or to fund campaigns. There was increasing partisanship and "too much effort being expended on one-upmanship, turf battles, and who was going to hold power." he said. "All of which obviates against working together and solving problems."

"By that time," Randolph Townsend recalled, "if you were an incumbent and did not tack right or left, your party would run someone against you in the primaries. That had never happened before." To help remedy this, Raggio instituted the Republican Senate Caucus, also called the Senate Republican Leadership Conference (SRLC). "We came up with a plan to go out and seek the best candidate possible to win seats," he explained. "We then would back that candidate from day one, regardless of the primary."

Townsend became part of that process: "It allowed us to run campaigns intelligently and no longer be dependent upon a party that was increasingly independent of us." Political donors now had the option of directly funding Raggio's SRLC rather than the Republican Party apparatus or the increasing number of political action committees (PAC) designed to promote particular agendas. Republicans were having a hard time raising money because of social issues. Companies and corporations did not want to alienate their employees or customers who might have various views. They preferred giving their money to individuals rather than PACs.

With the SRLC, they could utilize like-minded relationships to develop campaign funding to support their candidates. The SRLC, Townsend continued, did not care what a person's social philosophies were because "it was a waste of our time dealing with social issues." If the candidate were pro-life but running in a district where the electorate was heavily pro-choice, they would talk to them about the problems they would face in getting elected. "We never tried to change a person's position on such issues. A person should be able to believe what they want to believe," Townsend said. "The only thing Senator Raggio insisted on was that our candidates adhere to the basic Republican principles of limited taxation, limited government, free-market enterprise, and a belief in an individual's own capabilities."

Because this precluded so much infighting and wasted campaign funds within the party through the primaries, Republicans would maintain a majority in the Nevada State Senate for all but one of the subsequent ten biennial sessions. This feat required something besides a successful mechanism for funding and vetting candidates—that ingredient being a wise leader.

"Senator Raggio was able to train, mentor, and encourage us to be the best committee chairpersons possible," Townsend recalled. "That is crucial because it is where your policy comes from, and that is what campaign donors are looking for." He continued that these groups may not always agree with Raggio but always respected his knowledge of the budget and his ability to be fair and balanced. "Many who get power are only interested in maintaining it and jealously guarding their advantages," Townsend said. "Raggio understood that developing a better team made him a better leader."

Casino mogul Steve Wynn would agree. "Bill is one of the few people who has deep insight and a keen understanding of how the State works and how to balance the interests in the State." Wynn said he could sort through an incredible amount of information and identify what was important, but what was even more uncommon was his ability to function within a group with that kind of clarity and still be collegial. "It is a much more complex and deeper challenge."

Former Lieutenant Governor Bob Cashell had a more straightforward idea of why Raggio was so successful: "Bill understood he was not always going to get the whole pie, but he always made sure he got a slice. He knew he'd get the rest later."

5

The Republican Revolution

THE PHENOMENON OF THE 1994 national mid-term Republican sweep, which gave that party its first majority in the U.S. House of Representatives since 1954, played out in Nevada as well. On Election Day, the Assembly found itself with a twenty-one-to-twenty-one split, a curious situation that required two speakers and two chairs for each committee. In the Senate, the Republicans picked up two more seats, giving them a thirteen-to-eight majority.

Senator Raggio was again named majority leader by his caucus and passed out committee chair assignments. He told the press that he did not anticipate early partisan fighting and, indeed, bitter sectional issues, which had erupted during the previous session, were largely absent during the 1995 session. No piece of legislation could be approved without Raggio's imprimatur, and virtually every penny spent by the State required his blessing.

As Jon Ralston observed: "Rarely has Nevada had a lawmaker who could accomplish so much without saying anything. Raggio's very presence determines how legislation is written or not written, a barometer of what the governor and his comrades think they can pass through the Senate gatekeeper."[43]

Twenty years in the Senate taught him that the process only worked as a cooperative effort. His party, however, was headed in another direction.

*****

Fourteen years earlier, after Ronald Reagan was elected president, the political atmosphere in Washington, D.C., was surprisingly bipartisan. Reagan reached out to Democratic leaders like Senator Edward "Ted" Kennedy and Speaker of the House Thomas "Tip" O'Neill and cultivated working relationships with other Democrats in both houses of Congress. His first budget was opposed by Republican "New Right" senators but supported by "Blue Dog" House Democrats.

This geniality began to fray after the passage of the Economic Recovery Tax Act of 1981 (ERTA), designed to encourage economic growth, based on the theory of supply-side economics, which had traditionally called for lowering taxes for the wealthy to stimulate business investment, which would then "trickle down" to benefit society at large over the long term. This principle differed from the New Deal policies of Franklin Roosevelt, where the money was generally infused at the bottom and trickled up. At the same time, the Administration proceeded to dismantle a good deal of the federal government, called for the privatization of many of those services, and deep cuts to social welfare programs.

The president, Republican candidates for office, and radio talk-show political pundits increasingly hammered home the message that welfare freeloaders were fraudulently taking money from hardworking Americans. This message resonated with traditionally Democratic, male blue-collar workers.

In the "Republican Revolution" of 1994, the Gingrich-led House campaigned on the "Contract with America," the GOP won majorities in both chambers of Congress, gained twelve governorships, and regained control of twenty state legislatures. Gingrich was elected Speaker of the House and, within the first hundred days, passed every proposition featured in the Contract with America, including government and operational reforms, fiscal responsibility, crime, welfare, national security, small business incentives, and capital gains legislation—except for term limits for members of Congress.

This failure to enact congressional term limits would be a critical turning point in American politics because Republicans would now turn to state governments to enact such policies. As political gridlock became more prevalent in the national government, both parties increased funding in state races to secure their agendas.

However, Gingrich's national profile quickly proved to be of detriment to the Republican Congress. His unwillingness to negotiate with President Bill Clinton resulted in significant government shutdowns. Gingrich's uncooperativeness and perceived demeanor as a smug, antagonistic zealot diminished his popularity. As his ability to perform ebbed, Gingrich was ousted from party leadership and ultimately resigned from Congress in 1999.

*****

Baptist minister Jerry Falwell had delivered nearly 70 percent of the White, evangelical Christian vote to Ronald Reagan during the 1980 presidential election.[44] By then, Falwell's Moral Majority had become one of the largest and most influential lobby groups for evangelical Christians in the United States, and, according to Reagan's challenger, incumbent President Jimmy Carter, knew how to play campaign hardball: "A group headed by Jerry Falwell purchased $10 million in commercials on southern radio and TV to brand me as a traitor to the South and no longer a Christian."[45]

Falwell and others on the Christian right promoted prayer in public schools and the teaching of creationism and intelligent design theory in science classes alongside evolution. They opposed gun control, immigration, abortion, embryonic stem cell research, sex education, contraception, nontraditional gender roles, and non-heterosexual relationships. Randolph Townsend would later recall that, by 1984, with the arrival of evangelical Christian leaders as players in policymaking, many Republicans began to believe "God ordained them to run the country."

Another influential televangelist with a large following was Pat Robertson. Beginning as a faith healer, Robertson, a Yale University honors graduate and son of a U.S. Senator, amassed a fortune as a media mogul. Over the years, on his popular television show, the *700 Club*, Robertson has stirred up his audiences with wild claims. In 2001, along with Jerry Falwell, Robertson blamed terrorist attacks at the World Trade Center and Pentagon on the American Civil Liberties Union and "pagans, and the abortionists, and the feminists, and the gays, and the lesbians."[46]

Two years later, in 2003, the Supreme Court, in a 6-3 vote, struck down a Texas statute and ruled that public ideas about morality cannot justify infringing people's constitutional rights, recognizing that non-heterosexuals were entitled to constitutional protections for private, consensual, intimate conduct. This ruling further alienated fundamentalist religious communities with what they considered to be an overreaching abuse of power by the federal government.

The Christian right believes that the separation of church and state is not explicit in the U.S. Constitution; instead, activist judges in the federal judicial system have created such a separation. These judges misinterpret the Establishment Clause, which they hold was intended only to prevent the establishment of a state-endorsed religion.

Ryan Burge, a scholar of religion and politics at Eastern Illinois University and a pastor in the American Baptist Church, wrote in 2021 that in recent years, the lines between theology and ideology had become blurred: "The term 'evangelical' has broken away from its roots as a sub-genre of Protestant theology and has now morphed into a social, cultural, and political term that stretches far beyond the boundaries of Christianity." [47]

Christian support for right-wing politicians and the social policies they endorse is often best understood via the principles of Christian Nationalism rather than evangelicalism. Christian Nationalism asserts that the country was founded by Christians as a Christian nation, citing that Christians represent not only the largest religious population in the United States but the largest Christian population of any country globally, with nearly 205 million as of 2019.

Many believed they have a divinely inspired obligation to "take back" the country for God and that the federal government should declare the United States a Christian nation, advocate Christian values, not enforce a separation of church and state, allow Christian religious symbols in public spaces and prayer in public schools, and accept the belief that the success of the United States is part of God's plan.[48]

There would be no compromise, as Jesus had preached: "Whoever is not with me is against me." [49]

But, Bob Marcaurelle, interim pastor at the independent Mountain Springs Baptist Church in Piedmont, South Carolina, worried that with over two hundred Christian denominations in the United States: "When Christianity becomes the government, the question is whose Christianity?"[50]

*****

Republican ultraconservatives would benefit from the power of the Christian right within the American political system because of their extraordinary turnout rate at the polls. Along with high-volume voter turnout, they regularly attended political events, knocked on doors, and distributed literature, doing this election work with missionary zeal and rarely paid, a significant benefit to a campaign's bottom line.[51]

The radical right's mission to "take back" America became more manageable in 1987 when the Federal Communications Commission (FCC) Fairness Doctrine ended. This prompted an explosion of cable and satellite programming, which, unlike public media channels, did not have to base their stories on facts or present both sides of a question honestly, equitably, and with balance.

Political talk radio soon flourished, the most successful personality being Rush Limbaugh. With the Fairness Doctrine gone, Limbaugh began hammering on the driving principle behind a conservative movement that rose in the 1950s to combat New Deal government regulation of business, a basic social safety net, and broad publicly funded infrastructure projects. It was socialism, he warned, and was burdening hardworking white men trying to care for their wives and children with enormous taxes to benefit "lazy" people of color and free-loading feminists.

Liberals, he said, undermined traditional family values and the American work ethic, aided by corrupt "Big Government" tax-and-spend lawmakers. The theory was not new, but Limbaugh presented it in such an authoritative style, filled with passion and resentment, that

53

it resounded with his listeners as entertaining and redemptive. Limbaugh would become the most influential radio personality since Walter Winchell, who, during his post-WWII broadcasts, would often employ accusations against public figures as having ties to Communist organizations or sexual misconduct and use disparaging monikers to titillate his audience.[52]

Winchell's real power came from innocent people's widespread fear of becoming the target of his allegations. Limbaugh used similar tactics to build up his millions of dedicated followers, proving particularly effective in influencing Republican politicians.

By the end of the 1980s, more than 650 radio stations carried Limbaugh's show and a television program produced by Roger Ailes, who had packaged an unappealing Richard Nixon into a victorious presidential candidate in 1968 and would later head the Fox News Channel. As Limbaugh's accusations became increasingly untethered from fact and reality, he insisted his contracts with newspaper and radio employers required them to hold him harmless from any lawsuits resulting from his commentary.

Raggio would blame Limbaugh and others, like Sean Hannity and Glen Beck, for misleading audiences to the nation's great detriment: "These commentators and talk show hosts are entertainers. That is how they make their living."

Not everyone agreed. Nevada State Senator Ira Hansen, who had for years been a local media critic of Senator Raggio and other "establishment Republicans" through his newspaper opinion columns and radio talk shows, believed Limbaugh and Hannity were "brilliant guys." Hansen added that when he read mainstream media, he felt he was only getting one side of the story, and so people like Limbaugh were necessary to get the truth out. To critics like Raggio, who called them entertainers, Hansen replied: "Their only weapon against these pundits was unsupported ridicule."

6

At War with the Government

RUSH LIMBAUGH WAS AT THE HEIGHT of his popularity and political power in the mid-1990s when Carl Sagan, famed astronomer, author, and television science communicator, worried about the long-term effect this kind of packaged "feel-good" information would have on the future, anticipating a time when "awesome technological powers" are in the hands of a very few, and issues fuzzy: "Our critical faculties in decline, unable to distinguish between what feels good and what's true, we slide, almost without noticing, back into superstition and darkness."[53]

By the mid-1960s, after McCarthyites and Birchers had sown the seeds of government mistrust, suspicion continued over the ensuing decades with the unfolding of conspiracies and malfeasance on the part of high-level government officials, which began with the Johnson Administration's misleading information about the causes and conduct of the Vietnam War, later exposed after the publication of the *Pentagon Papers.*

The leaker of those papers, Daniel Ellsberg, became one of the smear targets of Johnson's successor, President Nixon, who approved operatives engaging in burglary, misuse of campaign funds, and other nefarious activities. These crimes eventually led to a cover-up within the White House, known as the Watergate scandal, resulting in Nixon's resignation.

Between 1978 and 1980, an FBI sting operation, code-named ABSCAM, led to numerous arrests for bribery and corruption, which included the criminal convictions of seven members of the United States Congress.

From 1981 to 1986, senior Reagan Administration officials secretly helped in the sale of arms to the Islamic Republic of Iran, despite a U.S. arms embargo, using some of the proceeds to fund a right-wing rebel group battling a leftist regime in Nicaragua, in violation of the Boland Amendment, recently passed by Congress, prohibiting aid to that group. Known as the Iran–Contra Scandal, several government officials initially impeded an investigation by destroying or withholding documents. Eventually, eleven individuals, including Secretary of Defense Casper Weinberger, received criminal convictions. Several of these convictions would be vacated on appeal due to legal technicalities.

Such deception by the Executive Branch would continue, with President Bill Clinton lying under oath about having an extramarital affair. Three years later, following the September 11, 2001 attacks on the World Trade Center towers and Pentagon, President George W. Bush's Administration, as a pretense to invade Iraq, repeatedly advanced "ties" between Saddam Hussein and Al Qaeda, and Hussein's alleged possession of weapons of mass destruction—all of which were later disproven.

Given all these scandals, it is understandable why so many Americans had lost trust in their government. Yet, this was merely the tip of the deception/misinformation/disinformation iceberg. Sociologist and political scientist Colin Crouch described the new template for American politics, where rival teams of professional experts tightly manage public electoral debate using new persuasion techniques. Manipulating the perception and belief of segmented populations by strategically using rumors and falsehoods blurred the distinction between truth and lies. [54] Carl Sagan had seen this coming and wrote prophetically:

> The dumbing down of America is most evident in the
> slow decay of substantive content in the enormously
> influential media, the 30-second sound bites (now down
> to 10 seconds or less), lowest common denominator
> programming, credulous presentations of pseudoscience

and superstition, but especially a kind of celebration of ignorance. [55]

Many news outlets' desire to appear impartial led to a "false balance," the practice of giving equal emphasis to unsupported or discredited claims without challenging their factual basis.

This process of claim and counter-claim provided days of quarrelsome news coverage at the expense of more profound analysis. It led viewers to identify emotionally with those who matched their image of an authentic, honest person. The rise of the Internet allowed people to choose their source of information, often entirely from like-minded individuals, reinforcing their opinions. Consequently, despite no factual evidence, a refrain often heard from those who believed in election fraud was that everyone they knew voted for the candidate who lost—so how else could that have happened?

In 2008, this new post-truth political model included a persistent belief that Barack Obama had been born in Kenya and so was an illegal president. Consultants who designed these types of attacks knew that, at the very least, it would send the accused off-message to defend themselves. The appeal and staying power of the "birther" element in the Republican Party helped strengthen other conspiracy theories: denying climate change, rejecting evolution, the safety of vaccines, and wild QAnon-inspired scenarios. Widely available evidence debunking these theories did not slow their growth.

For many, the concept of truthfulness in politics had become a source of mockery, creating a culture in which the new politics of public opinion and media narratives became disconnected from actual policy—the core of legislation.

Bill Raggio recognized that Nevada and the nation would suffer without sound public policy decisions. "They've built their base on disillusionment and cynicism." Raggio fumed. "They never have a plan or a proposal. They are never *for* anything— just *against* things."

*****

Since the time of inner-city, civil rights-related rioting in the late 1960s, an uneasy peace had prevailed. Many businesses destroyed and looted in the riots did not reopen, further depressing the local economy. Fearful whites had fled to the suburbs from communities adjacent to the rioting. Several intervening recessions in the 1970s-1980s and the loss of manufacturing jobs to overseas labor markets hit those in lower economic groups the hardest, further blighting inner cities and increasing the sense of hopelessness among residents.

In 1992, this relative tranquility shattered with the acquittal of several Los Angeles police officers on charges of savagely beating Rodney King, a black driver who, after a high-speed chase, had been arrested for drunk driving and resisting arrest. A bystander filmed the event, clearly showing King being struck nearly sixty times with police batons. Shortly after the verdict to acquit was reached, amid long-smoldering resentment at what they believed to be institutionalized police brutality against minorities by the Los Angeles police, rioting erupted in the South-Central area of the city. Film footage showed young black men pulling a white truck driver from his vehicle and beating him. As he lay defenseless on his back, he was slammed in the head with bricks and other objects as his attackers danced around him triumphantly.

President George H. W. Bush invoked the Insurrection Act of 1807, sending U.S. Marines in to assist the National Guard in restoring order. The rioting lasted six days, leaving 63 killed, over 2,000 injured, and billions of dollars in property damage.

The imagery of rampant stealing and property destruction and the televised beating of the driver had a profound, visceral effect on many white viewers, increasing the pace of White flight to the suburbs and, in the minds of many, validating right-wing talk show hosts, like Rush Limbaugh, that this was to be the fate of all Whites. Gun sales surged, and membership in right-wing militias spiked among those who believed themselves to be the last line of defense for white Americans against multicultural, liberal bureaucrats in the federal government.

In the wake of these events, Randy Weaver, an Iowa factory worker, moved his family to northern Idaho to escape what he perceived as society's corruption of American values. Weaver subscribed to an apocalyptic notion called "Christian Identity," which believed in the separation of the races and that Whites were the lost tribe of Israel. In August 1992, U.S. Marshals attempted to arrest Weaver at his cabin on Ruby Ridge under a bench warrant after he failed to appear on firearms charges. Suspecting a conspiracy against him, Weaver refused to surrender. After a gunfight in which Weaver's fourteen-year-old son and a U.S. marshal were killed, law enforcement laid siege to the cabin. An FBI sniper subsequently killed Weaver's wife.

Right-wing activists and neo-Nazis from a nearby Aryan Nations compound converged on Ruby Ridge to protest what they perceived as an unjustified federal government assault on a man protecting his family. Weaver surrendered nine days later, but the event reinforced in many and convinced others that they needed to arm themselves to fight the United States government.

In February of the following year, a similar scenario played out in Waco, Texas, when federal law enforcement officers stormed the compound of a religious cult called the Branch Davidians, who were awaiting the biblical apocalypse. Former members had told the FBI that their leader, David Koresh, was stockpiling weapons. When federal agents attempted to confiscate those weapons and arrest Koresh for firearms violations, a gun battle ensued, culminating, after 51 days, in a fire that destroyed the compound. Ultimately, 6 law enforcement officers and 82 Davidian members, including 25 children, died.

Clinton Administration Attorney General Janet Reno appointed widely respected former Republican Senator John C. Danforth to lead an investigation. Danforth's report cited "overwhelming evidence" that exonerated the government of wrongdoing. But right-wing talk radio hosts railed against the Democratic administration, especially Reno, for what occurred at Waco, fitting neatly into what was fast becoming a Republican Party narrative of an overreaching government out to crush individual liberties.

Limbaugh told listeners that the government's "murder" of its Christian citizens had been a strategy that Janet Reno devised, insulting her appearance as a traditionally unfeminine-looking, single woman—a classic "Feminazi." He further fanned the fears of his followers by implying, without proof, that the Administration's plan for declaring martial law was just around the corner.

After the standoffs at Ruby Ridge and Waco between armed citizens and federal government agents, membership in radical fringe militias continued to grow. These groups generally held libertarian and constitutionalist political views, strongly focusing on Second Amendment gun rights and tax protest. They also embraced many of the same conspiracy theories as predecessor groups on the radical right, particularly the New World Order theory, in which a cabal of powerful elites ruled the world through an authoritarian globalist agenda. Operating through front organizations, the Order manipulated world events and orchestrated political and economic crises to weaken and then topple sovereign states.

This conspiracy had long been a significant feature of radical conservatism, the villains changing over the years to include not just the U.S. government and non-Whites but, in their turn, Catholics, Mormons, Jews, Muslims, Freemasons, homosexuals, secular humanists, and bankers. A rehash of the centuries-old Illuminati conspiracy, most prominently led by televangelist Pat Robertson, viewed history as a conspiracy by a demonic force on the verge of total control. As such, antigovernment militant groups aligned with fundamentalist Christians must resort to all-out violence to save the world.

Such inflammatory rhetoric radicalized Gulf War Army veteran Timothy McVeigh. On April 19, 1995, a date chosen to honor the Waco standoff, McVeigh detonated a truck bomb at the Alfred P. Murrah Federal Building in Oklahoma City. The blast killed 168 people, including 19 children younger than six, and wounded more than 800. McVeigh was executed in federal prison for this crime in 2001.

By 1995, right-wing militias fancied themselves as protectors of American individualism in the face of an increasingly socialist government. These groups typically operated independently, using varying degrees of militancy and aggressiveness. Mistrust of government intentions was present in Nevada throughout the 1980s in the form of the so-called "Sagebrush Rebellion," which resisted federal land policy in Western states geared at conservation efforts. They also blamed powerful mining interests for depriving them of the use of grazing lands. As these Sagebrush rebels bridled under the lack of attention paid to their concerns, the dialogue grew more rancorous, with sporadic violence against government offices and employees.

It was not always the rural citizens who objected to federal overreach in the state. In the early 1960s, as a result of congressional committees investigating racketeering and the presence of organized crime in interstate commerce, Teamsters Union leader Jimmy Hoffa was sent to prison for defrauding the union's pension fund. Hoffa and his associates in organized crime had been primarily responsible for the development of Las Vegas by providing millions of dollars from the Teamsters Central States Pension Fund to develop hotel-casinos along The Strip, such as the Desert Inn, Caesars Palace, Stardust, and Circus Circus.

In 1961, U.S. Attorney General Robert F. Kennedy, who once acted as a special counsel to one of those congressional committees, saw Nevada as a Mob playground and set out to rid the state of corruption by establishing a federal criminal strike force with its primary mission to identify taxpayers and labor officials who derived substantial income from organized illegal activities. Their techniques included surveillance, search warrants, informants, and wiretaps.

Strike force activities would continue, at varying intensity levels, over the next twenty-five years. Even before the strike force arrived, Nevada was already home to more federal agents, per capita, than any other state in the nation. [56] Oscar Goodman, a Las Vegas-based defense attorney representing many of those accused of crimes by the strike force and later Mayor of Las Vegas, described the environment:

> It was a war down here during those days. Every day,
> day after day, there was a major search, a major arrest,
> a major subpoena issued. It was really the United States
> of America versus Nevada.

In 1971, about the time President Richard Nixon pardoned Hoffa, he offered Bill Raggio the position of U.S. Attorney for the District of Nevada to make up for betraying Raggio during his race for the U.S. Senate. Raggio's first point of reluctance to accept the job was that the strike force was too independent and would not be accountable to his office.

Many Nevadans, from the governor down, resented the heavy-handedness of the federal government and its evident disdain for the State's ability to handle its affairs properly and did nothing to quell suspicions among many Nevadans that the federal government was willing to overstep its authority when it pleased, helping anti-government fear grow into an instrument of political power.

7

Vanishing Cooperation

BY 1997, THE STATE LEGISLATURE could no longer kick education reform down the road, and it would turn out to be one of the most complex and controversial pieces of legislation ever to challenge lawmakers. Democrats and the influential teacher's union opposed some elements in Raggio's proposed Nevada Education Reform Act, so he did not get everything he wanted. However, because he had a history of cooperation on other issues with both groups and Democratic Governor Bob Miller, they had developed trust in him. Thought by many to be impossible, Raggio had advanced a conservative initiative with support from the teachers and Democrats. He later commented about the session: "I can't please everyone, but I try to call them fairly. I'm mindful of the dignity of the process."

An exuberant Governor Kenny Guinn would say: "It turned out we all had a friend in Bill Raggio." Not all agreed. Many in his party increasingly disliked and mistrusted Raggio as the political climate in Nevada continued changing with the national trend toward partisanship and non-cooperation. A growing ideological rift within the party would magnify the problem. All this converged as the thorny and traditionally heated task of reapportionment and redistricting in the 2001 session and was about to test Raggio's ability like no session before.

Nevada's rapid population growth over the past decade allowed it to form a third congressional district. Republicans and Democrats vied for an advantage in the new district, pressured daily by national party leaders intent on capturing the new seat for a House of Representatives with a slim five-seat Republican majority.

63

The election season began on an ominous note in April 2000 with a rift at the Washoe County Republican Convention. Several socially conservative delegates walked out because pro-choice activists were allowed to participate. Senator Raggio lamented this fissure: "I've been through many of these wars. The other party doesn't beat us. We beat ourselves."

In the wake of Speaker Joe Dini's retirement in 1999, new Assembly leaders would not be as dependable or, in Raggio's opinion, as honorable. He later recalled entering into an agreement with them that they would expand the Senate by two seats and by four in the Assembly: "But when we got into the actual negotiations on reapportionment and redistricting, I was informed that we had a problem with the redistricting on the Congressional seat we were adding in Clark County." Raggio felt the Democrats reneged on the promise to expand the State Legislature after they did not get everything they wanted in the creation of this new congressional district. Several years later, he was still "chagrined," saying, "I thought they had given me their word on that."

No compromise was reached before the end of the regular session. To complete the redistricting process, Governor Guinn called a special session to be convened on June 14, adding twenty-three additional measures for reconsideration. The special session lasted two days, and despite some foot-dragging by Assembly Republicans, a redistricting agreement was reached that would keep the Legislature at sixty-three members and provide a new congressional district evenly split between Republican and Democratic voters.

Republican Senator Mark James recalled Raggio's unique ability to work with members of both parties and reach across the aisle, despite his displeasure at Democrats going back on their word in redistricting:

> Senator Raggio provided leadership not just for the Republican side but for the Democratic side as well. I cannot imagine that there is a leader like him in another State Legislature that has so much respect across party lines.

Yet, shortly after the 2001 special session concluded, Republican State Senator Bill O'Donnell blasted Raggio in a story on the front page of the *Las Vegas Sun*. O'Donnell said he was leaving the Legislature when his term ended in 2002 because of members of the GOP caucus who failed to support him in his recent bid to wrest the majority position job from Bill Raggio and "bring control of the leadership position to the south."

"Legislators are more afraid of Raggio and more concerned with their own reelection than doing what is morally correct," said O'Donnell. He likened Raggio to dictators such as Joseph Stalin and Idi Amin, saying he ruled by fear and punished lawmakers like O'Donnell, who did not support him.[57] During the last days of the 2001 regular session, O'Donnell had surprised Raggio and other Republicans when he voted to block a Republican redistricting bill from passing out of committee. Ironically, that redistricting plan would have likely helped O'Donnell win reelection.

Senator Mark James defended Raggio, saying, "You never got that undertone that he had a personal agenda. When he was tough about an issue, he was doing it for the right reasons. And that's how he got us to follow him."

Joe Brezny, later manager of the Senate Republican Caucus, observed that it was all about compromise:

If they are smart enough to be tactical, the legislators
will take something back to the electorate. If they show
up as ideologues, going to change the world; not
tactical; starry-eyed; it is Senator Raggio's job to
remind them they have a constituency to care for.

In his nearly fifty years as a law enforcer and a lawmaker, Raggio dealt with vicious criminals, corrupt civic leaders and police officers, and inter-party and sectional opposition, which often manifested itself in smears and other attacks on his character. He weathered all of these with patience and dignity.

It would now be the turn of uncompromising, ultraconservative ideologues within his party to set upon him—and try to drive him from office.

*****

By the time Bill Raggio was elevated to the leadership of the State Senate in 1986, almost all these far-right fringe groups, many of them philosophically Libertarian, had aligned with the Republican Party as their political vehicle. Raggio probably did not realize initially that this new harsh tone of the party was anything but temporary, a burst of venting after years in the political wilderness. But over time, it became apparent it was here to stay.

Year by year, the rhetoric of national politics became harsher, eventually becoming standard within the Republican Party at the state level. In Nevada, Raggio increasingly became a target. A conservative activist circulated printed matter charging he was not a "real" Republican—rather a RINO (Republican in name only). Raggio's conservative credentials had never before been challenged. Ironically, many of these ultraconservative newcomers revered the memory of President Ronald Reagan. Yet, despite Raggio knowing Ronald Reagan, attending social functions at the White House during Reagan's presidency, and understanding and admiring his philosophy, he was branded less-than-Republican.

Of this, liberal journalist Dennis Meyers wrote:

Raggio was a solid conservative throughout his legislative years, though he never had much in common with those lawmakers who 'do not believe in government' and had latched onto the GOP as their political instrument. Raggio never confused their stances with real conservatism.[58]

Raggio had dispensed his share of political abuse at one time, but as a legislator, he had learned how to make his case without questioning the motives or goodwill of his opponents. Political pundits and others regularly associated the word "statesman" with his name. Raggio's consistent success in legislative accomplishment and strengthening the number of GOP officials had kept him relatively unassailable. However, the days when the art of consensus building was a respected tool of power were rapidly drawing to a close.

At seventy-three years old, it appeared it might be a good time to retire. The year before, 1999, had brought Raggio personal loss when his wife Dorothy died after a long illness. In addition, his legislative bedrock was shaken by the simultaneous retirements of longtime Secretary of the Senate Jan Thomas, reliable personal secretary Lucille Hill, and trusted Senate Fiscal Analyst Dan Miles. As if things could not get more complicated, his counterpart in the Assembly, Democrat Joe Dini, with whom he had developed unshakeable trust and respect, also retired.

Raggio had the knowledge, and that knowledge still equated to power. He was also concerned that those determined to replace him would create government gridlock, much to the detriment of Nevadans. He recognized the Legislature was poised on the brink of political, sectional, and philosophical divisions that would create chaotic, partisan infighting, the likes of which had never been seen in that body. Strong leadership could avoid that; no one else was ready to take the helm. The enactment of term limits was rapidly depleting the ranks of those who might have been able to do it. [59] His retirement would have to wait.

Republican and Democratic legislators had begun using considerable swaths of legislative time to hold regular caucuses behind closed doors to enforce party policy, a departure from when partisanship at the Legislature was understated, and strict party discipline was unknown. "It seems like they caucus on every vote," Raggio said. "We didn't do that in the past:"

> Once the election was over, everyone was willing to sit down and compromise, and now that's a four-letter word to some of these extremists. Those who obstruct don't belong in the process, whether they're

Republicans or Democrats. Legislation is still the art of compromise.

Raggio critic State Senator Ira Hansen would agree with him, saying that increased partisanship was primarily due to the caucus system. In this system, legislators gather behind closed doors, review the bills, and decide which they will support and which they will not.

"Back in the first twenty years of Raggio's time in the Senate," Hansen said:

> It was all done on the floor, where it was seldom partisan, with both Democrats and Republicans often disagreeing with those in their own party. In more recent years, with the caucus process, that kind of transparency is gone. When a majority agrees in caucus, despite those who disagree, they make it appear that there is no dissension.

If some Republicans did not like Raggio's traditional leadership style, Democrats watched in envy at his ability to get things done. Yet they were practical enough to know that such infighting would soon weaken the Senate's Republican majority—and open the door for them.

*****

President George W. Bush's administration began in 2000 after a campaign advocating "compassionate conservativism" in hopes of appealing to immigrants and minority voters. However, the platform failed to gain much traction among GOP members once his presidency began.

At first, the Republican Party remained reasonably unified with pro-government conservatives, comprising a significant group advocating increased government and an interventionist foreign policy. However, libertarian-leaning conservatives became increasingly dissatisfied with the GOP's stance on civil liberties, corporate welfare, and the rising national debt. At the same time, social conservatives began expressing dissatisfaction with the party's support of policies that conflicted with their moral values.

In Nevada, Republican Governor Kenny Guinn's popularity across party lines was evident in his overwhelming reelection victory over Joe Neal in 2002. In his State of the State address, Guinn called for nearly $1 billion in new taxes. He said it was time to stop putting off the tough decision and recognize that gaming and sales taxes alone, which comprised the bulk of the State's revenue, were not a stable enough base to continue to meet the needs of a growing State. "It is the only choice," he told the legislators. Inaction in the face of such a financial crisis would be "political cowardice."

The gaming industry has long advocated spreading the tax burden to other Nevada businesses, supporting a "margin tax" on business gross receipts and a sales tax on services. Most Nevada lawmakers agreed that, while gaming could pay more, it was dangerous to single them out. As one Democratic state senator from Las Vegas would later say, while it is "clear that gaming can afford to pay more," Nevada must broaden its sources of revenue: "The problem is nobody else pays anything. Until we can make corporations pay something, it's hard to ask gaming to pay more." [60]

Others, like Senator Ira Hansen, had severe reservations about gaming's share of the tax burden: "While I do believe gaming should have its say, after all, it employs hundreds of thousands of people in the State, I do not think it should be able to dictate tax policy to the Nevada State Legislature. That is where I draw the line."

Hansen would tell of how, years later, in 2015, when he became chair of the Senate Judiciary Committee, which dealt with most gaming matters, he received a telephone call from resort mogul Steve Wynn: "Not to congratulate me on being chair of the Judiciary Committee, but to tell me what to do, as in 'You will do this!'"

Gaming was, by far, the state's largest employer, and because its employees are unionized in Clark County, it provided workers with the ability to buy homes and raise families comfortably. But Hansen pointed out that it also created a large transit community that is expensive for education, social services, etc. Social costs were also associated with the business: gambling addiction, alcohol use, and sex trafficking. "It is an industry that encourages people to try to get something for nothing," Hansen added. "This is why the social statistics for Nevada are always at the top of everything bad and the bottom of everything good."

Hansen bridles at the argument that more mining tax will solve the problem. "There are probably four mines in the State that produce a hundred million dollars in profits. We need to tax industries that operate in the multibillions, and the only way to do that is with the gaming industry."

*****

Governor Guinn knew they could not keep kicking the can down the road to make it the next session's problem. So, he presented a plan for cutting the budget deficit by increasing taxes on businesses, live amusement, cigarettes, and alcohol. Guinn also proposed a property tax of fifteen cents per hundred of assessed value. Such a move, he said, would stabilize Nevada's revenue structure in the future. Guinn said the time for relying on cuts in existing programs to fill the budget gaps was over: "I refuse to balance the budget on the backs of our children, senior citizens, and the poor…this is the time for courage and leadership."[61]

During the session, Bill Raggio married Dale Checket. Following their wedding in a Catholic church in Carson City, Kenny and Dema Guinn hosted the civil ceremony and reception at the Governor's Mansion and acted as the official witnesses. But there would be no immediate honeymoon, as the level of discord between Raggio and what he termed ultraconservatives within the senate's Republican caucus was nearing the breaking point.

This widening split in the Republican caucus resulted from Raggio's decision to join Republican Governor Kenny Guinn and over two-thirds of the Legislature in voting for a tax increase to keep Nevada schools open. It was a tough choice, Raggio said, but necessary because Nevada's children deserved to be educated.

After the State spent nearly $4 billion in the prior budget cycle, Guinn proposed spending almost $5 billion over the 2003-2005 biennium—a period for which the Economic Forum was projecting revenue of under $4 billion. While lawmakers generally liked Guinn's vision for dramatically increasing the size and scope of State spending, many of his fellow Republicans balked at his centerpiece plan for a proposed gross-receipts tax on business.

Due to a 1996 voter-approved initiative, the Nevada Constitution required a two-thirds supermajority in each legislative chamber to approve tax increases. That meant fifteen members of the Republican Assembly caucus would control the minimum number of votes necessary to block new taxes. Quickly earning the nickname "The Mean 15," they unanimously rejected the governor's tax proposals

These "no tax" individuals presented a new challenge for Raggio as a "closer." For the first time, he faced a legislative bloc within his party that refused to negotiate. Mark James was also exasperated: "They refused to think that far ahead about how the State will function. If you see these people in debate or interviews, they really do not have solutions or understanding."

He said Raggio was the most fiscally conservative person in the state but would not allow Nevada to go bankrupt. "We did not have any choice," James added: "Are we going to let people out of prison? Are we going to close schools? If we do not fund these services, the judiciary will step in and dictate how we spend these funds."

Senator Raggio asked the "no tax" bloc what they would accept. "Their reply was always that they would cut expenses," James said. "When asked where they would cut, they usually replied in generalities about government waste, but the fact is, they will never put their finger on anything specifically."

Governor Guinn agreed that people who vote "No" or "Yes" on everything are not good legislators. "The problem in 2003 occurred when people like Assemblyman [Lynn] Hettrick and Assemblywoman Angle did not provide alternative plans. They would vote 'no' on tax plans other people submitted but wouldn't offer a plan themselves."

Not all Assembly Republicans took that stand. Assemblyman Joe Hardy, from Boulder City, was a physician who had benefited from the State's educational system by attending Sparks High School and premed at the University of Nevada. He understood that the educational system required adequate funding to meet the state's future needs.

He polled his fellow Assembly members to determine their budgetary "bottom line." Armed with that information, he prepared a list of eighteen items that he wanted to include in the budget. The following month, coaxed by fellow Assemblyman Josh Griffin, he went to Raggio's office with his plan in exchange for his vote on a tax increase. As a new Assemblyman, he was a bit intimidated by Raggio's reputation.

Hardy explained to Raggio why he was there and handed him the list. Raggio, who had seemingly memorized every line item of every budget over the years, went down the list, telling Hardy which items he would agree to and which he would not. Hardy agreed, and Raggio asked him what his cap "bottom line" was. Raggio then picked up the phone, called the Legislative Counsel Bureau Legal Division, responsible for drafting the legislation, and told them to include Hardy's figure. The freshman assemblyman was stunned at how quickly Raggio had negotiated for his vote.

Hardy's deal with Raggio not only infuriated Assembly and Senate Democrats, who were against the budget cap Hardy proposed, but his fellow Republicans, as well. "They kicked me and Josh Griffin out of the caucus," he later said, "so we were not privy to what they were doing."

8

The No-Tax Pledge

TOWARD THE END of the Reagan presidency in the late 1980s, taxes had been a fundamental issue with ultraconservative Republicans. Grover Norquist, head of Americans for Tax Reform, created the "Taxpayer Protection Pledge" and encouraged incumbents and candidates at all levels of government to sign it. The pledge version for state legislators states that the signer will "oppose and vote against any and all efforts to raise taxes."[62]

Political pundit Steve Sebelius wrote of those who took the pledge:

> It's a fair bet none of them even considered any other course. That doesn't make them courageous, smart, or good legislators. It just makes them inured to reasonable counterarguments. And in the end, it made them wholly irrelevant, because who needs to negotiate with those who cannot compromise, especially when they comprise a minority of a minority?[63]

But conservative journalist Chuck Muth disagreed, saying the pledge signers were not irrelevant. "The power of the pledge isn't so much in an individual signing the pledge, but in electing a sufficient number of pledge signers to thwart any and all efforts to increase taxes." Even though six of the ten Republicans in the State Senate signed the pledge, when all ten united as a bloc to oppose the extension of the sunsets for the previous tax hikes, they were, Muth said, extremely relevant because most of the session, tax hikes were dead, thanks to unified opposition:

> And if just two of the four Senate sell-outs had kept their word and opposed extending the sunsets, there'd have been no extension of the sunsets. If there are eight pledge signers in the Senate, the tax-hiking side can't get the two-thirds supermajority it needs to raise taxes. It's simple math. [64]

Far-right Senator Ira Hansen disagreed with him on this issue. When he first ran for office in the State Assembly in 2010, Muth pressured him to take the tax pledge. He refused and never did take it.

"I told him that there may be a time when it would be necessary to raise taxes," the former Eagle Scout later said, "and I would want to be able to keep my word. I do not think an elected official should commit to something like that on a national or state level." He added that it was even more critical at the state level because Congress can spend more money than they have at the national level, but the state cannot.

Hansen's intuition was correct in that every tax pledger in the Nevada State Legislature, including Sharron Angle, would break the pledge. Even Chuck Muth, Hansen said, who pressured these legislators to sign the pledge, would eventually take $20,000 from the Sands Corporation to lobby for building a $2 billion football arena in Las Vegas. "Call it what you want, but it was a tax. The ultimate violation," Hansen said of Muth, echoing Bill Raggio's sentiment that it would make hypocrites of them all.

Ultraconservative Republicans and Libertarians had railed against Raggio for not taking the pledge and because he advised his political colleagues not to. "It's time to quit the bluster," he replied, pointing out that, contrary to what some political candidates claimed, citizens of Nevada were not overly taxed. "According to the Tax Foundation," he said, "we are the second, only to Alaska, in having the nation's lowest tax burden per capita. We don't have a state income tax or corporate income tax, yet I got chewed up for saying we're not over-taxed."

However, those who took the pledge received considerable support. Michael Bowers points out in his book, *The Sagebrush State*, that, as of 2003, Nevadans were "virtually obsessed" with their taxes despite Nevada having one of the lowest state and local tax burdens among the fifty states.

The majority of Nevada voters, he wrote, were so fearful of having their taxes raised that they amended the Nevada Constitution to prevent the State from collecting inheritance taxes from the estates of deceased individuals, even though this provision also precluded the State from picking up its share of the federal estate tax. "Nevada was the only state not to do so and lost millions of dollars in taxes that reverted to the federal treasury."[65]

This repeal of the estate tax would go into effect in 2005. Raggio objected because that money was traditionally earmarked for higher education, which he felt was an appropriate investment in Nevada's future. This loss of revenue would leave a gaping hole in the State budget that would have to be filled either by moving money from other programs or drastic cutbacks.

Eventually, the Governor's 2003 budget, which included some tax increases, passed in the Senate by the required two-thirds majority but did not pass in the Assembly. The governor ordered a special session, then another. He had worked with the Senate to approve an $870 million tax plan. Assembly Republicans promised to ensure a two-thirds majority if the plan did not involve more than $800 million in taxes. A frustrated Senator Raggio suggested that lawmakers who want such drastic cuts in social and health spending should visit clinics for the mentally and physically disabled. "Go out and look at those clinics, look at the kids on the waiting list, and your heart will burst," he said.

The Assembly could not muster a two-thirds majority. State Attorney General Brian Sandoval, a former Republican Assembly member, testified in committee that lawmakers would violate the State Constitution if they failed to pass a balanced tax-and-spend plan by July 1, the beginning of the fiscal year. When asked, Sandoval admitted he had no idea what the punishment would be for lawmakers who violated that constitutional tenet.

When July 1 arrived, the State was without a budget. Governor Guinn then took the extraordinary step of suing the Legislature for violating the Nevada Constitution by failing to approve a balanced budget and appropriate funds for public education by the beginning of the new fiscal year.

On July 10, 2003, the Nevada Supreme Court ruled on the case of *Guinn v. The Legislature of Nevada.* Chief Justice Deborah Agosti handed down the court's decision in a vote of 6-1, stating that Nevada's public educational institutions were in crisis because they were unable to proceed with preparations for the coming school year due to the impasse that has resulted from the procedural and general constitutional requirement of passing revenue measures by a two-thirds majority. They found in favor of the governor, saying that the procedural requirement "must give way to the substantive and specific constitutional mandate to fund public education."

A flurry of legal motions was filed in State and federal courts on behalf of twenty-four Republicans from the Assembly and Senate, petitioning the Nevada Supreme Court to rehear its July 10 decision. "I do not agree with the court's analysis," Bill Raggio said, promising to personally not support any State budget that did not receive a two-thirds majority.

On July 22, an $836 million compromise tax package for funding the public schools and State government received a two-thirds vote in both houses of the Legislature. Final approval was assured when Republican Assemblyman John Marvel of Battle Mountain voiced his support for what he admitted was an imperfect tax plan. Marvel would give the tax plan the two-thirds supermajority in the Assembly. "We must uphold the Constitution," he said. "I think it raises too much tax, and I think the appropriation is too high, but if we're going to do the business of the State of Nevada, I reluctantly say I will vote for this bill."

Marvel would later recall:

I get charged now with being a tax-and-spender, but my motive for that was to get our schools open. My vote was for the kids, not for raising taxes…it was the right decision. As far as I'm concerned if you're going to be a statesman, be a good one. It turned around and got me in the end [Marvel would lose reelection in 2008], but at the same time, it was for the right reason.[66]

When asked about the chain of events, Raggio was furious. "It was a farce. Four legislative leaders would meet, and we would get an agreement. Assembly Minority Leader Hettrick would agree and sign off on it but would then come back and say he could not get his caucus to support it." What needed to be emphasized, he said:

Is that we weren't talking about whether or not to raise taxes; we were only talking about the difference in amount over the two-year period. This is all lost in the discussion and their historical recall. They are all out there today saying they would not raise taxes. That is simply untrue.

Raggio was appalled, less by the tactics than by the attitude of disrespect for majority opinion—and the hypocrisy. Democratic Assembly Speaker Barbara Buckley agreed, saying, "They are not, as they claim to be, 'no tax' people; they just disagreed with Senator Raggio on how much." In 2009, Guinn would say, "Everybody can argue about it now, but what kind of shape would the State be in today if we had not done that? It would be devastating." The session had further infuriated Raggio because three of his caucus members, Senators Anne O'Connell, Sandra Tiffany, and Barbara Cegavske, reneged on their promise to him near the end of the session and voted differently. Republican Senator Randolph Townsend, another caucus member, recalled how incredulous Raggio was for a long time afterward, that "they could look him in the eye and tell him they would do one thing, and then go do something else."

Raggio later commented that the three "fought me tooth and nail on the tax issue and refused to discuss it... O'Connell abstained when it came to a vote, and the two others voted against it."

"We should've done this together instead of this political posturing all the time," Raggio said. "Too many people are more concerned about how they are viewed on personal issues than how well they govern."

According to former Legislative Counsel Bureau Director Lorne Malkiewich, Raggio would frequently attend training sessions for new legislators to share his vast experience, always ending with a discussion on what he considered to be the most important lesson of the day—not losing the trust of others by going back on your word:

> If a legislator gave his or her word too easily, Raggio told them, they would find themselves left with two equally bad options: To continue following through with a bad piece of legislation or go back on their word —irreparably damaging their reputation for dependability. It was particularly egregious to Senator Raggio in 2003, when such a lapse of integrity involved three veteran senators.

In Nevada, no single issue did more to divide the Republican Party than tax increases.

9

Incivility

BY 2004, ULTRACONSERVATIVES controlled the apparatus of the Nevada GOP, which resulted in incumbent Republican senators Ann O'Connell and Ray Rawson being defeated in the primary by even more conservative candidates, Dr. Joseph Heck and Bob Beers, both of whom went on to win the general election. [67] Senator Townsend believed the loss of O'Connell and Rawson could have been prevented: "If they had asked us for our help, they would've won that race. It was totally unnecessary. We lost two twenty-year senators in one day."

As a result of their equivocation about the amount of tax increase that they would support in the previous regular session, resulting in two special sessions and a lawsuit, costing taxpayers over $500,000 in administrative costs, the State Assembly Republican caucus would lose five members in that election. Despite much of the original "Mean 15" bloc surviving, Raggio acknowledged that the process would probably run more smoothly in the Assembly now that the Republican minority was smaller, and early signs of that were evident when a bipartisan plan for property tax relief was subsequently enacted.

Support for an effort by some southern Nevada Republican senators to oust Raggio from his leadership position did not materialize. He would also remain as Chair of the Committee on Finance.

Raggio would appoint newly elected Senator Bob Beers, a member of the Assembly Mean 15 the year before, as vice-chair of the Finance Committee to allow him to make hard decisions on spending, now that it was his responsibility. Observers like Claire Clift, Secretary of the Senate, felt that this made Beers more moderate because he was now in a leadership role and had to come up with workable solutions rather than just identifying problems. Senator Warren Hardy agreed, saying anyone charged with making such tough decisions would never be as critical again.

*****

After the 2005 session ended, Las Vegas Review-Journal journalist Ed Vogel interviewed Governor Guinn, who responded to criticism by Assemblywoman Sharron Angle for his having increased the size of state government. He noted, with irony, that all legislators still in office who had resisted his tax plan in 2003 would eventually vote for the budget in 2005—a budget that was 23 percent larger than the previous one. "Even Assemblywoman Angle voted for the record budget."

Raggio later noted, "While some partisanship occurred of necessity on some issues, there was an air of civility between leadership, legislators, and the executive branch, which has seriously deteriorated."

Much of that deterioration resulted from widely trusted Governor Kenny Guinn reaching his term limit on January 3, 2007, and being replaced by Republican Jim Gibbons, a former U.S. Congressman. State Senator Dina Titus won the Democratic nomination in 2007 to run for governor and handily won highly populated Clark County. But that margin was insufficient to overcome Gibbons' support in the rest of the state. Bill Raggio later remarked that because of Titus's comments years earlier during the fair share controversy, calling Washoe County "a sponge," resentful voters outside of Clark County would make it difficult for her ever to win a statewide office.

After listening to the new governor's State of the State address, Democratic Assemblywoman Sheila Leslie commented on how the dynamics had shifted: "You have a very experienced Legislature and a governor who has been in Washington for ten years. The political

80

climate is very different here. While Washington is filled with partisan sniping, we must work together in Nevada to find solutions."[68]

While public relations problems plagued Gibbons before he was elected governor, he battled lawsuits, investigations of political wrongdoing, and a messy divorce from his wife, Dawn, following his election.

Years later, Ben Kieckhefer, who would serve briefly as Governor Gibbons' Press Secretary, disagreed with Leslie's assessment that the Washington culture had tainted Gibbons:

> I would not blame it on D.C. Jim struggled, not with
> decision-making, but with the spotlight that comes with
> the office, versus being one of 435 people in the House
> of Representatives. I believe D.C. is far more infected
> by politics now than when Jim Gibbons was there.

Democrats now held a twenty-seven to fifteen seat edge in the Assembly—one short of being "veto proof." A demonstration of unconcealed partisanship occurred in the first moments of the new legislative session when freshman Republican Assemblyman Ty Cobb, who occupied the seat formerly held by Sharron Angle, defied legislative custom by loudly voting "no" during a roll call vote to seat Barbara Buckley as Speaker of the Nevada Assembly. Leadership members are chosen by their parties and then ratified by votes on the Assembly and Senate floor. In the interest of civility, previous ratifications had traditionally been unanimous.

Buckley, the first woman speaker in the Assembly's 142-year history, later commented that she did not take it personally but that Cobb's gesture did not bode well for the freshman. "People who lack a sense of judgment sometimes run into trouble with legislation because they don't reach out to people," Buckley said. "You can't do anything unless you get a majority. It doesn't matter if you have the best ideas."

In the State Senate, Democrats picked up another seat when longtime Las Vegas educator Joyce Woodhouse upset Sandra Tiffany.

*****

By mid-April 2008, Bill Raggio had no Republican challengers in his reelection campaign. Then, just moments before the closing deadline for filing for elective office in Nevada, former Assemblywoman Sharron Angle arrived at the Office of the Secretary of State and filed to run against him in the primary election.

The fifty-nine-year-old Angle attended public schools in Reno and later obtained a Bachelor of Fine Arts from the University of Nevada. For the next twenty-five years, she worked as a substitute teacher in Ely, Tonopah, and Reno and taught art for five years as a lecturer at Western Nevada Community College in Winnemucca. Angle, previously one of the Mean 15, served in the Assembly from 1998 through 2005. While there, she prided herself on her unwillingness to compromise on almost every issue.

While working to cultivate an image as a conservative maverick, Angle's dogmatic approach caused her to have a difficult time drawing other legislators to her issues. A fellow Assemblywoman, Sheila Leslie, would later say:

> She took great pride in voting 'no' for everything. We have some very conservative people in the Assembly, but she was the only one voting 'no' on a technical cleanup bill. The lobbyists didn't talk to her, and the legislators wouldn't talk to her. When you vote 'no' on everything, no one wants to deal with you. [69]

Raggio was disappointed to learn Angle had filed at the last minute to challenge him in the primary election. "I thought her credentials were minimal," he said. "She served four terms in the Assembly and during all those years was of absolutely no consequence." "Over the years," he added, "she has always been more interested in her personal success than in helping to solve issues."

*****

Before he could fully concentrate on the campaign, Raggio faced the daunting task of helping resolve a gigantic shortfall in the

State's budget. After the Legislature had to reduce the State's Rainy-Day Fund to a mere $632,516, Governor Gibbons called for a special session in June 2008. Then nothing happened. Days passed with no guidance on what Gibbons wanted the legislators to do now that they were back in Carson City.

The governor's lack of leadership confounded Democrats. Speaker Buckley said: "The governor is saying he believes we have a budget crisis but is proposing no solutions to deal with it. I find that ludicrous. To now just abdicate his responsibility to come up with suggestions to ensure a balanced budget just defies logic."

Buckley was grateful, however, for Raggio's presence in the decision-making process, calling him "an honest and dedicated public servant" and commending him for working with her toward a bipartisan solution.

Although the governor had been at odds with legislative leaders, Ben Kieckhefer admired what he saw, saying that even in the political discord swirling around them, Buckley and Raggio were able to bring together two-thirds of both houses to override the wishes of Governor Gibbons and his vetoes. "An amazing feat:"

> Barbara is pretty much universally respected by people on both sides of the aisle. I think she and Bill worked together as well as any two legislators that body ever had—maybe better than the legendary relationship between Raggio and Democratic Assembly leader Joe Dini. [70]

*****

At the end of the special session, Raggio turned his attention to Sharron Angle's political challenge. He knew that the Democrats would make a decisive run statewide and nationally in 2008 and was not pleased that such divisiveness weakened the Republican Party.

Angle's cheery smile and engaging presence proved successful when asking for door-to-door voter support. Many in her camp thought that the eighty-one-year-old Raggio would not be up to competing

83

with her at that level, especially during the heat of summer. They would soon be proven wrong.

Bill and Dale began spending their mornings canvassing the district. On any given day, numerous volunteers assisted them, including State Republican Party Chair Sue Lowden and her husband Paul, former Governor Guinn and his wife Dema, and Reno Mayor Bob Cashell. Later, Raggio would jokingly speak of how Governor Guinn's popularity made him ineffective as a precinct walker because when surprised residents saw who it was at their door, they would invite him in and offer him a beer. "So, he didn't cover much ground," Raggio quipped.

The campaign energized Raggio, and he was delighted by the support he received from groups that did not usually endorse Republican candidates, such as the teachers' union and the National Education Association. Such endorsements were fodder for Angle's campaign, which used it against Raggio as "proof" that he was not a true conservative. Raggio replied:

> I'm not going to tell people not to endorse me. Her lack of endorsement speaks for itself. Her only endorsement was from what I call the Ron Paul group, which, in effect, makes her a libertarian who has chosen to wear the Republican label. In many ways, this is a fight for the soul of the Republican Party in Nevada.

Even the nuns at the Carmel monastery in his district, realizing Raggio was in a close race, volunteered to change party affiliation from Democrat to Republican so they could vote for him in the primary election. When Raggio heard about it, he humorously reassured them, "It's only a venial sin (as opposed to a mortal sin) to be a Republican."

Part of Angle's campaign strategy was to convince Republican primary voters that, for all Raggio's influence, the northern part of the State had not fared well during his tenure. Her campaign was strongly supported by a conservative PAC that advocated the tax pledge, declaring that Nevada had a spending problem, not a revenue problem—and Raggio was responsible for that. [71]

Rather than discounting these charges against him, Senator Raggio embraced them as an opportunity to remind his fellow lawmakers that they were elected "not just to serve Republican or Democrat constituents but in the best interest of all the people of Nevada" and that inflexible political positions, pledges, and narrow, overly simplistic answers for solving the broad and complex issues facing the State, were an abdication of their duty to vet information and make informed, thoughtful decisions.

He refused to allow his flexibility in bargaining with the Democrats to be restricted by dogma and called Angle's anti-tax message "dishonest." While she had voted against all the major spending bills in 2003 as part of her opposition to the tax increase, Raggio reminded voters that she did vote "yes" in 2005 on each of the budget bills, breaking her tax pledge while approving spending measures in *excess* of the 2003 budget. "I don't call that conservative," Raggio said. "I call it hypocritical."

Her campaign ads repeated the message that a person with principles would never compromise. Raggio was incredulous: "If that were true, you would never end a legislative session. Yet, people listen to her and believe that diatribe."

He recognized the Angle campaign was appealing to those who treated programmatic matters, like spending and taxes, as moral issues rather than public policy issues, and so considered compromise not as a necessary legislative tool but as ethically wrong, saying, "I've had to deal consistently with a house of the other party:"

And we would have gotten nowhere if we were not willing to compromise. If we were going to put good and evil labels on things, we might as well not have shown up. Legislation is the art of compromise, but there is no compromise in their minds. It is either all their way or the highway.

10

Unwinnable Races

In August 2008, despite the extreme right wing of his party's effort to oust him, Bill Raggio won the Republican primary election with just over 50 percent of the vote.

Greg Brower, who had lost his Assembly seat to Sharron Angle in the 2002 Republican primary election, observed that Raggio recognized the Tea Party was "picking up steam" within the Nevada Republican Party and could not take any chances in the primary election. "It did not matter," Brower said, "that he had all the money and all the endorsements and a reputation for legislative accomplishments because these fringe voters in the Republican primary didn't care about any of that:"

> They were angry with Bill, resented him, and really did not like him. So, Bill campaigned on identifying Republicans who would not skip the primary and who actually showed up. His campaign was converting Democrats, even nuns, to change their registration and vote for him.

Joe Brezny directed the campaign's day-to-day operations. In addition to funds, endorsements, and a legion of volunteers and campaign workers, Brezny utilized the services of a Nevada firm specializing in high-tech campaign strategies, targeting voters who, if they showed up at the polls, would likely vote for Raggio.

"One reason Senator Raggio won," Brezny said, "is because he was smart enough to surround himself with the best." One of those "best" was his friend and trusted advisor, Greg Ferraro. Ferraro had known Raggio since he began lobbying at the Legislature in 1989. The two bonded. As the 2008 election cycle neared, Raggio turned to Ferraro to oversee the general operation of the primary election campaign, focusing his talents principally on the message, polling, and spending.

Ferraro would later say of that campaign:

> His opponent's attacks were mostly personal, the subtext being that because of Bill's age, he would not have the vigor to mount a successful campaign. We did not respond on that level, nor did we panic even when the poll numbers closed a bit, as they do in every election. Instead, we decided to prove that Bill was strong and energetic.

Ferraro recalled that Raggio worked harder than anyone, out every day, regardless of the summer heat, walking precincts in his district and working well into each night making calls and writing letters. "Republican voters want to see a candidate not only with energy and desire but also someone with the ability to get things done," Ferraro said. "He won because he is Bill Raggio."

Reflecting on Raggio's political career, Ferraro added:

> In November 1970, Bill lost a tough race for the U.S. Senate. One of the great ironies is that voters made a choice that, in fact, turned out to be a very good one. Had it not been for that, Nevadans would be bereft of the Carson City master who, empowered by the giant spirit of his small State, set the course for the Nevada we know today.

Three days after his primary election victory over Sharron Angle, Raggio commented that, while he had experienced competitive elections over his career, he had never faced an opponent as deceptive as Sharron Angle or where his record was so distorted and his reputation so besmirched. "It is very apparent to me," he said, "that she will stop at nothing to further her own personal ambition."

✳✳✳✳✳

With the departure of Dina Titus from the State Senate, thirty-five-year-old Democratic State Senator Steven Horsford of Clark County, a relative newcomer to the body, was elevated to Senate majority leader. Horsford's meteoric rise to the top leadership position was primarily the result of his drive and savvy as a political operative. The latter resulted in his receiving credit for having helped engineer the election of two relatively unknown Democratic Senate candidates in upset victories over conservative Republican incumbents Bob Beers and Joe Heck. Their defeats resulted in the Republicans losing their majority in the State Senate for the first time in sixteen years.

Many observers, including Senators Raggio and Townsend, felt resources that could have helped boost those Republican incumbents in the November election had been needlessly depleted during the summer to fend off Sharron Angle's challenge in the Republican primary.

But, Raggio had to concede that it might have still been an impossible task because the Democrats had all the money they needed nationally and, through the efforts of U.S. Senate Majority Leader Senator Harry Reid, had more money than they needed in Nevada. "Money poured into the State," Raggio said, "particularly to unseat southern Nevada candidates Heck and Beers. There was nothing we could have done to win those races."

Greg Brower later recalled how disappointed Raggio was, now stuck with a "rookie Democratic majority leader" inexperienced and unskilled in the legislative process and living with the knowledge of how avoidable it was if the right-wing fringe had not infringed on nominating process procedures and prevented the party from selecting "electable candidates."

Raggio felt that, because of the far right's influence, there had been a significant defection of registered Republican voters to become non-affiliated. In addition, the Libertarian Party insisted on running candidates that drew votes from the Republicans. He was also chagrined with right-wing TV and radio hosts whom he considered "entertainers" rather than purveyors of honest news and were tearing his party apart for ego and personal profit:

> Rush Limbaugh, Hannity, and the like spent six months, day-by-day, hour-by-hour, skewering [2008 Republican presidential candidate and U.S. Senator] John McCain because he was not conservative enough and wasn't a "real" Republican. Yet, at the end of the presidential campaign, they expected their listeners to vote for McCain. A lot of them did not vote for him or support the party because they had been traumatized for six months.

McCain graduated from the U.S. Naval Academy in 1958. As a naval aviator, he was shot down in 1967 on a bombing mission over North Vietnam, breaking both arms and a leg. As a POW, he was regularly beaten and subjected to psychological torture. Given the opportunity to be released because his father was a high-level naval officer, McCain chose to stay with his fellow POWs. Finally, released in 1973, McCain left the Navy and, in 1982, was elected to the U.S. House of Representatives from the State of Arizona. In 1986, McCain was elected to the U.S. Senate, succeeding Arizona native, a conservative icon, and 1964 Republican presidential nominee Barry Goldwater.

While generally adhering to conservative principles, McCain also had a reputation as a "maverick" for his willingness to break from his party on specific issues. His stances on LGBTQ rights and gun regulation were more moderate than those of the party's base. He was also known for his work in the 1990s to restore diplomatic relations with Vietnam. He made regulation of political campaign financing a primary issue, resulting in the passage of the McCain–Feingold Act in 2002, which was unpopular with hardline conservatives.

The 2008 presidential race pitted the seventy-two-year-old McCain against a younger, fellow U.S. senator, Barack Obama. McCain's strategy was not well-articulated from the start. He did not distance himself early or convincingly enough from unpopular President George W. Bush.

Party strategists also pointed out that his lack of a coherent economic message loomed large after a financial crisis exploded in September 2008, one of the worst in the nation's history, and all but erasing his lead in the polls. His late choice of running mate, Alaska Governor Sarah Palin, brought out far-right voters but alienated just as many independents, who viewed her as unqualified and unintelligent.

Yet, some political observers suggested that McCain lost the race on October 10, 2008, about three weeks before the election, when he engaged in a spontaneous act of civility that infuriated ultraconservative voters. During a televised town hall question-and-answer forum with voters in Minnesota, a woman prefaced her question by stating, "I can't trust Obama. I have read about him, and he's Arab." McCain interrupted her by politely taking back the microphone while sorrowfully shaking his head. The act was spontaneous, without strategic precaution. "No, ma'am," McCain replied. "He's a decent family man, a citizen that I just happen to have disagreements with on fundamental issues. That's what this campaign is all about."[72]

McCain's failure to demonize his black, Democratic opponent did not comport with the new GOP temperament. As Bill Raggio would forlornly observe, these new hardline conservatives no longer considered McCain a "real" Republican who never had a chance of winning the election after his "No, ma'am" reply.

*****

The 2009 Legislature convened on Monday, February 2. Following the previous session, relations between Governor Gibbons and Democrats had deteriorated rapidly. Revenues were falling, and economic forecasts were dire. In the interim, the governor had called two special sessions to deal with the revenue shortfalls, and lawmakers had been able to agree on reductions without raising taxes.

After submitting his Executive Budget, which included a 36 percent cut in higher education and a 6 percent cut in salary and benefits for teachers and State workers, and then threatening to veto any legislation that contained new or increased taxes, Governor Gibbons went into isolation. This was a far different approach than his predecessor, Kenny Guinn, who was in the Legislative Building almost daily, often testifying before legislative committees on behalf of measures he supported. Gibbons was rarely seen, provided no leadership, and had little relevant input. Instead, he sent his staff to testify.

Raggio immediately criticized the budget cuts as too draconian. By now, most legislators, including much of the Senate's Republican Caucus, which traditionally would be working to implement a Republican governor's budget, had become indifferent to the Governor. Like everyone in the Legislative Building, they knew that Senator Raggio held the real clout in the party, and it would be up to him to help resolve the $2.3 billion budget crisis. Raggio began working with the new majority leader, Senator Steven Horsford, and Speaker Barbara Buckley in the Assembly.

While Assembly Democrats held a veto-proof majority, Senate Democrats would require at least two Republicans to vote with them to reach the two-thirds majority necessary to override a veto. The final decision would be in Raggio's hands, though he downplayed the notion early on. "I'm going to do precisely what is necessary in the best interest of the State," he said. "That's what I was elected to do and not to represent my party or any special interest group."

Raggio insisted any tax increase would require an automatic expiration date, called a "sunset provision," to be revisited in the following session. "If the economy improves and we don't need them, then they'll be gone," he explained.

Another of his conditions for accepting a temporary tax plan was "a credible, objective tax study" conducted by an independent consultant to be completed by the following legislative session. That way, "there will be something that the public can understand, whether or not new taxes are needed, tax increases are needed, and whether we are spending the money wisely on essential services." If those conditions were met, Senator Raggio said, then he and at least one other member of his caucus would vote for the plan, thus giving the Senate enough votes to override the governor's veto.

The Nevada Constitution grants the governor five business days to act on a measure from the Legislature. If that period elapses without any action, the measure will automatically pass into law. With the legislative session mandated to end June 1, lawmakers must have the appropriation measures to him no later than 5:00 p.m. on Friday, May 22.

Majority Floor Leader Horsford was now confronted with a difficult task: keeping the Republican caucus happy for the two votes he needed. His legislative inexperience was frustrating for many. Despite occasional meltdowns, the tight deadline generated a bipartisan spirit throughout the session. However, all the hard work nearly came undone with high drama rarely seen in the Senate Chambers. Desperate anti-tax forces attempted to use rumors of potential conflicts of interest to peel off "yes" votes. Their targets were Senators Warren Hardy and Bill Raggio.

Hardy was first on the "hit list." The potential conflict arose because he was President of the Associated Builders and Contractors, on whose board sat the Greater Las Vegas Chamber of Commerce President, Steve Hill. The Chamber was lobbying assiduously to curtail public employee pay, benefits, and collective bargaining. Because Hill technically acted in a supervisory position over Hardy, the senator said he would abstain from voting on the public employee measure on the advice of legislative counsel and with "an abundance of caution." About six hours later, the Nevada Supreme Court unanimously voted that the State Ethics Commission, an Executive Branch board, be barred from action against Hardy based on the constitutional doctrine of separation of powers. The court ruled that only the Legislature could determine whether its members could vote on an issue or if they must disclose potential conflicts of interest before voting. Hardy was gratified by the ruling, "assured there won't be an unfair, politically motivated attack on their ability to vote."

Raggio then announced that he would abstain from the crucial tax package vote. Unbeknownst to him, an attorney from the law firm of Jones Vargas, where Raggio was a partner, testified earlier in the session on the tax bill, and Raggio had just learned that he might be threatened with an ethics complaint as a result. He then gave an impassioned speech, decrying such attacks on the integrity of legislators, saying, "I will abstain. I will do so reluctantly because my first obligation here, under the oath I took, was to do what's right for the State."

He added that outside activists were seeking to thwart the tax package, especially the Western Alliance Fund, a conservative PAC airing radio ads opposing the tax increases. Raggio ended his speech by defending the ideal of citizen-legislators while pointing out how increasingly untenable that concept was becoming.

As expected, Senator Raggio proposed his amendment to provide a firm two-year "sunset" on most of the tax package and to have a "credible" tax study performed before the next session. It failed to pass in a voice vote. Raggio would not change his conditions, and Senator Hardy, the second vote needed by the Democrats, agreed not to vote.

The deadline to have the legislation at the governor's office was now within an hour, and tension on the floor and in the gallery was palpable. Realizing Raggio would not allow him even a small victory, Horsford relented with precious minutes ticking away. As amended, the bill carried seventeen to four, with five Republicans voting for passage.

Just six minutes earlier, in another part of the Legislative Building, Assembly Speaker Buckley interrupted comments on the tax measure and called for a vote. It passed twenty-nine to thirteen. When comments about the bill resumed, Republican Assemblyman John Carpenter of Elko County asked to speak. He had been one of the

Mean 15 who defied tax increases in 2003 but was now the only Assembly Republican to back the 2009 tax measure.

Because of term limits, this would be Carpenter's last session. He told his colleagues that the vote had been the most challenging decision in his twenty-two years as a legislator. "My own children and grandchildren have received fine educations," he said, "and all children in Nevada should have an opportunity for quality education."[73]

Jon Ralston later wrote that the "real travesty" had been in the way many Republican legislators, "using simple-minded, fatuous rhetoric," had voted against a tax increase, but only after voting hundreds of millions of dollars in spending for K-12 education and the overall spending package. This tactic forced lawmakers to cut critical services affecting children, families, and older adults. They supported education, Ralston said, "but hypocritically opposed the revenue package to fund it…this is the worst kind of craven and disingenuous behavior."[74]

Speaker Barbara Buckley would later say:

> If you watch the struggle of factions within the Republican Party, Senator Raggio is clearly of the old school, an old-school Republican who believes he can be conservative without being so traditional that you forget why you have government in the first place. He is very pragmatic. He is not going to be swayed by people who govern by sound bite; that is not true governing.

Those who knew of Raggio's contributions to the people of Nevada were troubled by the malicious nature of mounting attacks on him. He survived a 2009 effort by ultraconservatives to recall him because he had broken a campaign promise not to raise taxes. Raggio admitted that during the campaign, he said he would not want to raise any taxes but soon found out that, due to the recession, State revenues were far short of what anybody could have imagined, saying: "We saw that it would decimate education, health, and human services and public safety if we did not raise some revenues. So, I committed early that we would determine what essential services were needed through the budget. We made deep cuts."

He added that Nevada was at a point where it could not cut anymore "unless we want to start firing State workers, taking wheelchairs away from the disabled, closing rural clinics, and making people wait five years for mental health treatment." Further cuts to the prison budget could not be made without endangering society. Even if legislators were willing to take responsibility for dismantling State programs, he said, federal law would prevent it. That was the reality.

Former Governor Guinn agreed: "When people say they want smaller government, they just don't understand what they mean by government." He gave the example of Clark County voters approving bond issues to build more schools but would not fund teachers. "People want very tough crime laws, but they do not want to pay for policemen or prisons," he said. "Some say, 'I don't want government,' but they do not really think what government is. This problem cannot be solved with all cuts or all taxes."

Governor Gibbons did not veto the final legislative agreement in 2009 and had to defend his "no tax" promise. The governor said he had to accept increasing fees because it was part of the compromise, later admitting when the interviewer pressed that "a fee is a tax" and acknowledging breaking his no-tax pledge. [75]

For having accepted the revenue increases in the compromise, the no-tax zealots denounced the governor, effectively losing what remained of his dwindling political base. The Nevada anti-tax group Citizens Outreach spokesman declared that the governor's "non-stop parsing and telling of falsehoods about breaking the Pledge were worse than breaking the Pledge itself." [76]

Raggio would later say:

In the end, the revised budget was passed. Eight Republicans voted no; however, my perception is that most of them, as in 2003, secretly hoped it would pass, and they could claim they didn't vote for it. It is another example of voting to get reelected rather than doing what is necessary in the best interest of the State.

*****

After decades of frustration, the Republican right-wing rank-and-file flocked to the emerging Tea Party and its anti-establishment message. Senator Ira Hansen, who identified strongly with the Tea Party, described the political roller coaster ride to get there, saying that, with the election of Richard Nixon and his running mate Spiro Agnew in 1968, their hopes were renewed that the Goldwater days were back. But with the indictment of Agnew for corruption and Nixon's resignation after the threat of impeachment over the Watergate scandal, the administration was brought down. Nixon's immediate replacement, Gerald Ford, steered the party away from hardline conservatives. He selected moderate Republican Nelson Rockefeller as his running mate and was defeated in the subsequent presidential race by Jimmy Carter.

The 1980 election of Ronald Reagan, Hansen said, seemed to have brought right-wing Republican conservatives back to power. Still, ultra-right hopes were soon dashed when Reagan selected as his running mate "the ultimate Washington establishment insider," George H. W. Bush. With the subsequent presidencies of both George H. W. Bush and George W. Bush, rightist conservatives felt they had been "stabbed in the back" because both men had campaigned using "conservative platitudes" about not increasing taxes or expanding government—yet both did so once in power, as Reagan had.

Hansen observed that Bill Raggio identified most strongly with Ronald Reagan, but Reagan represented "big government and compromised conservative values." This distinctly libertarian perspective often—and oddly—overlapped with the same message as Social Democrats at the other end of the political spectrum.

"At the time the Tea Party came along," Hansen said, "Raggio had been in power about thirty years, and there was a sense that change was needed in the party leadership. The balance of power that had worked pretty well for that leadership did not work well for rank-and-file Republicans, the Goldwater Republicans, the Taft

96

Republicans, the Nixon Republicans, and the Reagan Republicans." This conservative wing, he said, represented the majority of the party.

Hansen said the anger against Raggio came about because when he and other Republicans were elected and re-elected, they consistently did the bidding of the "establishment" Rockefeller element of the party, adding:

> In all the pictures you saw of Raggio, he was with high-power gaming lobbyists like Jim Joyce and Harvey Whittemore. These are the power guys in the State of Nevada. Raggio was right there with them, which is why the Tea Party eventually directed such hostility and animosity against him.

All this eventually forced the GOP to walk a tricky line between maintaining its policy positions and fostering the loyalty of an energetic base pointed in a different direction. While the Tea Party was ostensibly centered on government spending, in reality, it exhibited a broad cultural opposition to a changing country and its newly elected president, Barack Obama. Race, societal change, and the threat of violence by heavily armed militias were a constant undercurrent within the movement. [77]

11

Raggio's Rubicon

IN 2010, JIM GIBBONS pursued reelection for governor despite having a popularity rating of just 10 percent, the lowest in the history of the office. On June 8, he made more history by being the first incumbent governor since statehood to be defeated in his own party's primary election, losing to the former Assemblyman, State attorney general, and federal court Judge Brian Sandoval.

Just before the Republican primary vote for a nominee to face U.S. Senator Harry Reid, Raggio voiced his concern:

> Both parties have extremists, and it brings out the worst in a lot of people. I find it difficult to believe that the majority of Americans want that kind of polarization in our political process. God forbid Sharron Angle becomes a Republican nominee for the U.S. Senate. I would never support her. I know her, and I know she is treacherous and deceitful and will do anything to win.

He would soon be disappointed when Angle won the bitterly fought Nevada Republican primary election, capturing 41 percent of the vote. Her primary challenger, Sue Lowden, came in second with 26 percent. Lowden was an early favorite and consistently led in statewide polls as the one candidate who could defeat Democratic Senator Harry Reid. She had been a State senator and Chair of the Nevada Republican Party, with prior experience as a businesswoman, television news anchor, and kindergarten teacher.

Political observers attributed her surprising loss to several factors, such as votes siphoned off by another candidate, Danny Tarkanian, and some highly publicized gaffes. She also faced attacks on her qualifications and the hostility of Clark County's largest labor union, which had long-standing issues with her casino-owner husband. In addition, the Reid political machine interfered with potential support and donations to her race, fearing she would present a more formidable challenge to him than Angle. As one observer explained, lobbyists instinctively dreaded alienating a Senate majority leader, and "Reid is quite a mean guy about this stuff. It is very personal."[78]

Bill Raggio was deeply disappointed, not only because he felt Lowden was well-qualified, but by the unusual coalition that worked against her, saying:

> She lost the primary to Angle, largely through efforts of both Reid campaign strategists and the likes of the national Tea Party Express, Club for Growth, and similar ultraconservative operations who chose to endorse and fund Angle—a strange combination, to say the least!

Raggio added about the GOP primary process: "Most people are not that interested in politics until general election time. So, these ultra-conservatives made themselves delegates to a county or state convention and took control of the party machinery."

This dynamic was evident two years earlier, in April 2008, when the Nevada State Republican Convention was called off without electing national delegates to the presidential nominating convention. It was a frustrating culmination to a long day that had pitted GOP establishment supporters of the presumptive presidential nominee, Senator John McCain, against an insurgency who backed former Libertarian Party candidate Ron Paul.

Irate Paul supporters believed the "establishment" was exerting its power to shut them out. Nevada Republican Party Chair Sue Lowden disagreed, "I'm the only [state party] chairman in the entire country that allowed him [Paul] to speak at the convention," she said. "I want people included in the Republican Party, not just one kind of Republican, but all kinds of Republicans." Those who arrived would not be as accommodating to her.

*****

Tea Party and other ultraconservative candidates also benefited from a recent landmark U.S. Supreme Court decision earlier that year in the case of *Citizens United v. Federal Election Commission,* holding that the First Amendment right to free speech applied to independent expenditures for political communications by corporations, including nonprofit corporations, labor unions, and other associations. The ruling immediately led to well-funded political action committees called Super PACs. The *Citizens United* ruling would prove to have a more positive effect on the electoral success of Republican candidates than Democrats.

David and Charles Koch, former members of the John Birch Society, who had made billions of dollars in the oil refining business, used their collective wealth and connections, especially in the wake of the *Citizens United* decision, to gain powerful political influence. Their donations of hundreds of millions of dollars pushed the Republican agenda towards their libertarian, free-market bent, giving rise to the Tea Party movement changing the American political landscape.

The Koch brothers helped shape the country's climate change policy. Through their organization, Americans for Prosperity, they donated hundreds of millions to elect Republicans who would vote against environmental protections. At one point, they influenced hundreds of members of Congress to sign a pledge to vote against any climate-change legislation that did not include equivalent tax cuts.

A month after Sharron Angle's nomination, former Governor Kenny Guinn unexpectedly died at seventy-three. Randolph Townsend would recall:

When Kenny died, it left Bill as titular head of the Nevada Republican Party. But that is a completely different job than legislating and would have required Bill to be constantly out traveling, fundraising, and building up interest. Raggio had no time to do that because of his other duties, and frankly, he was no good at it.

Kenny Guinn had been Bill Raggio's strongest ally in the struggle to prevent the State's Republican Party from sliding into extremism. Now, Raggio would have to do it alone.

*****

In the weeks leading up to the general election, Sharron Angle, an evangelical Christian-right conservative in a State whose major population center boasted the label "Sin City," was surprisingly well ahead in most polls. This success was even more astonishing because of her radical views during the campaign: She called for Social Security and Medicare to be "transitioned out" in favor of privatization and opposed the fluoridation of drinking water.

During her short time in the Assembly, Angle prided herself in voting "No" on almost every issue before the body—as a protest against the system. It played well with her political base of ultraconservative Tea Party[79] adherents who felt that "establishment" Republicans no longer represented them or their principles.

Raggio was equally troubled that the Tea Party attracted more radical elements hitching a ride to political power within the Republican Party, described by a pundit in 2010 as:

An uneasy conclave of Ayn Rand secular libertarians and fundamentalist Christian evangelicals; it contains birthers, Birchers, racists, xenophobes, Ron Paulites, cold warriors, Zionists, constitutionalists, vanilla Republicans looking for a high and militia-style survivalists.[80]

101

This scenario was all too reminiscent of conspiracy-driven John Birch Society adherents whom Raggio, alongside notable Nevada Republican Paul Laxalt, had struggled, with some success, to sublimate at the State level during the 1960s. The resurgence of such factions, he said, was now driving away all who disagreed with them. As such, a year before the Reid-Angle race, Raggio had publicly warned against underestimating such a movement. "I have seen this before," Raggio said. "We should take this seriously."

Seventy-year-old Harry Reid had spent his early years in the hardscrabble mining town of Searchlight, Nevada, and moved to Henderson for high school. He graduated from Utah State University in 1961 with a double major in political science and history. While attending George Washington University Law School, he worked as a Capitol police officer. Upon his return to Henderson, Reid gained experience as the city attorney and was elected to the Nevada Assembly in 1968.

In 1970, he was elected lieutenant governor of Nevada, serving alongside Governor Mike O'Callaghan, his former high school teacher and boxing coach. One of the duties of the lieutenant governor is to preside over the Senate floor meetings, which he did in Bill Raggio's first session in that body. He moved on to the U.S. House of Representatives in 1982 and the U.S. Senate in 1987. Reid ascended to Majority Floor Leader in 2007—arguably the second most powerful individual in the United States.

Raggio recalled Reid as an effective president of the Nevada State Senate. "Harry was very low-key and non-confrontational. He was quiet and kept to himself, and I recall seeing him often jogging alone around Carson City to stay in shape."

By October 2010, the Reid and Angle campaigns had reached an extraordinary level of venom. Few could recall a race where so much of the electorate disliked both candidates. Understanding Angle's propensity for gaffes, Reid had operatives follow her to events and meetings to record her.[81] Angle recognized she was sometimes her own worst enemy and limited her availability for questions to local and national media. She later explained why to a *Las Vegas Review-Journal* reporter:

We needed to have the press be our friend. We want them to ask the questions we want to answer so that they report the news the way we want it to be reported. The way to ruin a conservative is to pass them off as part of the radical fringe. They always try to marginalize me.[82]

Yet, her positions on various issues mirrored those of radical fringe groups. She believed that the U.S. Department of Education was unconstitutional and should be eliminated, saying that education was best controlled as close to the local level as possible. She did not believe the U.S. Constitution mandated the separation of church and state. In a June 2010 radio interview broadcast statewide, Angle opposed abortion, even in cases of rape and incest, saying it is against "God's plan."[83] She favored eliminating the Internal Revenue Service code and abolishing the Federal Home Loan Mortgage Corporation.

Angle did not accept the premise of humans contributing to the creation of global warming, saying there was no sound science to back that up. She believed the U.S. should withdraw from the United Nations because it is a bastion of liberal ideology and "the umpire on fraudulent science such as global warming."[84]

She accused those in Congress who disagreed with her of being "domestic enemies." On a local, right-wing radio talk show, she said: "I hope that's not where we're going, but you know if this Congress keeps going the way it is, people are really looking toward those Second Amendment remedies." [85]

Angle's campaign advisers worked hard to soften her image as an extremist, but her inability to refrain from making outlandish remarks made that impossible. Asked to comment on the latter, spokesman Jerry Stacy said via email: "Sharron Angle does not advocate a revolution. Her goal is to go to Washington with other like-minded elected officials who understand the proper role of the federal government as already defined by our Constitution."[86]

The issue that appealed most to her voters was their nativist fear and suspicion of immigrants. In a slate of attack spots, Angle had claimed that her Democratic opponent, Reid, favored "open borders" and "amnesty" for illegal aliens— actions that would allow insidious elements into the United States. The commercials contained images of scowling, bandanna-clad men with dark complexions and footage of similarly menacing-looking figures sneaking around fences.

Many voters in Nevada were equally disenchanted with Harry Reid, who had become a lightning rod for anger about the worsening recession. By mid-to-late 2010, the severe decline in the State's construction and tourism industries had left nearly 200,000 out of work and looking for jobs. Including those who had given up looking for work, the actual jobless rate in Nevada was more than 20 percent of the workforce, nearly rivaling figures from the Great Depression in the 1930s. The State also had the highest home foreclosure rate in the nation, and that figure was rising.

Reid's low-key personality, which had already earned him a reputation for being a cold, calculating political animal, was now viewed by many as a sign that he was unsympathetic and detached from their problems. His biographer Jon Ralston wrote:

> He just didn't have time or the temperament for social niceties or for the self-editing mechanism most politicians have. But the caricature of Harry Reid—the former boxer who was not afraid to land a low blow, the ruthless tactician who would do anything to win, the charismatically challenged curmudgeon—is so one-dimensional.[87]

Republican former State Senator Ben Kieckhefer saw another reason for Reid's perceived aloofness:

> What you have to remember about Harry Reid is that when you are the Majority Leader of the United States Senate, the second most powerful person in the country, and you have responsibilities that go along with that level of power, influence, and significance, you become somewhat disconnected sometimes from where you come from.

Not to say that Harry Reid ever forgot about Nevada, and I think he used his position to help the State significantly, but sometimes his attention was elsewhere. And that's okay.

Republicans had beaten up Senator Reid on almost every issue over the previous two years, and political observers gave him only a slight chance of winning reelection against any viable Republican opponent. The selection of Angle, however, gave Reid the opening he needed.

Frustrated by the absence of that "viable" GOP challenger and fully conscious of Angle's lack of qualifications, the 200-strong "Republicans for Reid" list was established, containing some of the State's most influential lobbyists and businesspeople. Reid also received endorsements from such high-visibility Republicans as Wayne Newton, former First Ladies Dawn Gibbons and Dema Guinn, former Lieutenant Governor Sue Wagner, and Reno Mayor Bob Cashell.

Nevadan Sig Rogich, founder of R&R Partners, former U.S. Ambassador to Iceland, and White House advisor to both Presidents Ronald Reagan and George H.W. Bush, spearheaded the effort and, putting partisanship aside, would later say Reid was likely the most important elected official in Nevada history in terms of what he was able to achieve. An Angle victory, he added, would not only deny Nevada the most powerful position in the U.S. Senate but untold millions in earmarked federal funds for Nevada that went hand-in-hand with such power.

Asked what inspired him to form Republicans for Reid, Rogich recalled a dinner discussion with Senator John McCain. McCain represented the State of Arizona bordering Nevada along the Colorado River and warned Rogich: "You're going to have a big issue with the Colorado River potentially. You better make sure that Harry's at that table."[88]

Several top Republicans endorsed Sharron Angle, including former Congresswoman Barbara Vucanovich, former Nevada Secretary of State Dean Heller, Nevada Congressman Mark Amodei, and former Governor Bob List. List dismissed Reid's Republican supporters as just a few people with economic or personal ties to Reid and his agenda. Nevada's largest newspaper, the *Las Vegas Review-Journal*, also endorsed Angle.

Bill Raggio explained his reasoning for endorsing Harry Reid in a statement released on October 7, 2010, saying only one candidate, Senator Reid, had sought his endorsement. He had not heard from Sharron Angle or talked with her since long before she decided to run against him for the State Senate two years earlier. As a lifelong Republican, Raggio espoused the words of President Reagan, never to speak ill of other Republicans. "In other words, she should quit calling dedicated people like former Governor Guinn and many other good Republicans, RINOs, and other derogatory terms."

His inability to accept her extreme ideas and positions did not, in themselves, preclude an endorsement. However, coupled with remarks she had made in a secretly taped conversation disavowing the Republican Party and saying it had "lost its standards and principles," did. "For all these reasons," Raggio said, "I am unable to support Sharron Angle."

He qualified his decision by saying that he was not pleased with, or supportive of, many of the issues that Senator Reid had advanced and had told him so. "I believe he understands that he must vote more strongly to represent the views of his Nevada constituency in the future," Raggio said, "rather than a liberal agenda which many feel drifts toward socialism in America."

Raggio added that he opposed most of President Obama's agenda. "Barack Obama is not president because of how I and others like me voted. I voted for Senator McCain, who lost in large part because ultraconservative voices bashed him for a year leading up to the election." He concluded: "I truly believe most Nevadans, and for that matter, most Americans, are disgusted with negative campaigning and would like to see civility restored to the political process, with both parties working together and seeking responsible compromises in difficult and complex issues."

Raggio asked his friend and advisor Greg Ferraro to review the statement before release. Upon considering the political consequences of the message, Ferraro suggested he make a few minor modifications, and will never forget the unequivocal reply: "Don't change a word!" [89] Ferraro later said that Raggio never joined the "Republicans for Reid" group, despite it containing numerous luminaries within the State Republican Party, because he felt he needed to send a more powerful message.

12

The Soul of the Party

SHARRON ANGLE'S CAMPAIGN responded to Raggio's endorsement of Reid, calling him a "Good old boy career politician who does not believe in Republican principles." [90] Of all the notable Republicans who endorsed Senator Reid's reelection, Raggio became the lightning rod for far-right backlash. During the remainder of the impassioned campaign, the media either applauded or vilified him almost daily for his stance.

Interest in this race extended far beyond Nevada, and Angle's hopes stayed strong as the result of an eye-popping $14 million haul in campaign contributions between July and the end of September, much of it from conservative PACs outside the State that had come to see her race as increasingly winnable. Indeed, Reid and Angle would each spend over $20 million on their campaigns to sway a relatively small number of the 1.1 million registered voters in Nevada (of whom 723,000 would turn out).

On November 2, Reid defeated Angle by 40,000 votes, a margin of nearly 6 percent. Five days later, Raggio described the 2010 Nevada and national mid-term election as the most angry and uncivil he had witnessed since he first voted in 1948.

Republicans recaptured control of the House of Representatives, increased their seats in the Senate, and gained a majority of governorships. The Tea Party faction within the Nevada Republican Party was now one of the most powerful and organized of any state, nearly knocking off Senator Raggio two years earlier and coming within six percentage points of defeating the majority leader of the U.S. Senate.

Nationally, upsets occurred in races traditionally secure for Democrats, such as the election of Tea Party-endorsed candidate Scott Brown in Massachusetts for a U.S. Senate seat held for decades by the Kennedy brothers. Two years after the 2010 *Citizens United* decision, *The New York Times* declared that Tea Party lawmakers were no longer a fringe of the conservative coalition but now "indisputably at the core of the modern Republican Party."[91]

In Nevada, Brian Sandoval won the governorship handily. Congressman Dean Heller won, and former State Senator Joe Heck defeated Dina Titus in her bid for reelection to Congress. As Senate Minority Floor Leader, Raggio spent the campaign trying to focus his efforts on adding Republican seats in the State Senate to regain the majority, as well as supporting Republican candidates for other State and local offices, circumventing primary elections, which, Raggio said, "are divisive, costly and aid the other party."

In 2009, taxpayer pledge proponent and political pundit Chuck Muth wrote that Raggio and members of the Senate Republican Caucus met, as was their custom, to interview candidates to decide their endorsements in the upcoming election. However, unlike years past, Muth stated, the endorsement process now had a philosophical litmus test: The Taxpayer Protection Pledge: "The anointment process is complete, and the lines are drawn for next year's battle royale for the soul of the Republican Party. It will be the Raggio Republicans vs. the Conservative Republicans." [92]

Yet, when the election ended, all but one of the Raggio-endorsed candidates won.

Raggio had long recognized that because the time between the September primary election and the November general election was so short, the damage Republican candidates did to each other could often not be repaired in time for the election. The ferocity of the primaries seemed to be increasing as party unity disintegrated into heated debates over social issues, such as abortion, school prayer, and gun control. Wealthy donors, pushing ultra-right social agendas and favorable tax policy, were now circumventing Raggio and his previously successful method of selecting winning candidates via the

Senate Republican Leadership Conference's focus on traditional Republican policies of small government and pro-business.

Moderate and traditionally conservative voters in both parties rarely participated in primary elections, assuming that the mechanism would select the best candidate to represent their needs. Most believed that the general election was the most important to participate in. As such, increasingly fringe groups passionately dedicated to a particular cause came out for the primaries and worked for primary candidates who would represent them.

In many areas of the country, these groups participate in party primary elections more out of concern for political purity than for winning the general election. Incumbents who appeared willing to make the kinds of compromises that allow governing to happen were often rejected at the primary level and replaced with someone who refused to engage with the opposing political party. Such threats of being "primaried" were usually enough to turn an incumbent, who had been previously willing to negotiate, into an uncooperative ideologue.

Rather than pay more attention to primary election candidates to end this cycle of intimidation in both parties, dissatisfied voters became more apathetic or changed their affiliation, often becoming nonaffiliated voters, who, in most states, cannot vote in primaries. Thus, the most motivated, often fringe elements, worked hard to turn out that vote in their favor. In a State like Nevada, Greg Brower said, because moderate Republicans, or even traditional conservative Republicans, traditionally did not vote in primary elections, they "abdicate the decision to the right-wing fringe." [93]

To help change this dynamic in primary elections, Republican State Senator Ben Kieckhefer filed a statutory initiative in his last session to create open primaries. Kieckhefer noted that when there is a system in which 30 percent of the electorate decides how the election comes out, the remaining 70 percent in that district are ultimately insignificant in the outcome of that election and have no voice in who represents them in the government, "it is a system that has problems:"

> Closed primaries create a disincentive to public officials who would otherwise be willing to work on

issues, try to find compromise on issues, and make bad bills better. If someone says the system is working, they have a vested interest in it. It just seems awfully acute right now.

These primary candidates were—at first—essentially unelectable in general elections. Still, as time passed and the political and cultural line between the two major parties became more defined and conflicting, the rise of a blind, almost tribal, political partisanship would carry the day.

In mid-November 2010, the Nevada State Senate Republican Caucus voted to end Bill Raggio's tenure as the party's floor leader. He was unsurprised, saying he had heard of "some Republican Party groups threatening our Republican State senators with retaliation if they did not vote to replace me."

The caucus elected Northerner Senator Mike McGinness as the new minority leader and Southerner Senator Barbara Cegavske as the assistant minority leader. McGinness acknowledged that Raggio probably lost his longtime role as caucus leader because of his support for U.S. Senator Harry Reid in his recent campaign against Republican Sharron Angle. He added that this was not Raggio's only move that upset Republicans. His support for increasing taxes, particularly in the 2003 and 2009 sessions, had angered many in his party, both north and south, who did not forget. [94]

Others saw another underlying reason for Raggio's removal from leadership. Senator Anne O'Connell later recalled that during the raucous 2003 debate over tax increases, Raggio had stepped in and essentially stripped authority from Senator McGinness, then chair of the Committee on Taxation. "He usurped the power of the Tax Committee," declared Senator O'Connell. "I always felt very badly for Mike McGinness, who chaired the Tax Committee. It was a big insult to take the chairmanship away from him. That really started a division in the caucus."[95]

Raggio agreed with her recollection of events:

> Mike McGinness did feel that he had been usurped, but it was a matter of necessity and not one of having confidence in him. I just reached a point where we were into a special session and had to get something done.

Another factor that may have contributed to the change of leadership was a smoldering, decades-long resentment, since at least the time of the fair share issue, that Raggio, as majority leader and chair of the Finance Committee, provided more favorable funding to those in the northern part of the State.

Many felt that the funding of the Highway 580 extension between Reno and Carson City was a recent example. At that same time, other funds were directed toward the Highway 11, Colorado River bridge project in the south, but an uneven share. One particularly costly piece of the Highway 580 project was an exceptionally high and expensive viaduct that soon earned the disapproving title of "Raggio's Bridge."

Randolph Townsend (in whose state senate district the bridge was built) said: "The decision to go with the bridge was made solely by the Nevada Department of Transportation chief. Raggio had no input."

Senator Joe Hardy later said that many in southern Nevada always felt Raggio got more for the North, which was aggravated by the fact that the population in the South had grown so much in comparison. Yet, the fact that Raggio's replacement was not from the South indicated it was not a compelling factor in the decision to change leadership. "It was not the bridge that got Raggio," Hardy added. "It was his stand on taxes in the face of a rising anti-tax element in the party. If anything, the bridge was a footnote to the whole dramatic process."

Hardy was in an excellent position to know this because, as a member of the Republican caucus, he attended the meeting that ousted Raggio. As a freshman Assemblyman in 2003, Hardy had risked his budding political career bucking the party caucus on the issue of taxation to save education in Nevada. As a newly elected senator, he would again go against the majority of his caucus, this time to retain Bill Raggio as minority floor leader.

Raggio and Hardy had won each other's mutual respect during that challenging 2003 session, and Hardy had not forgotten how Raggio accommodated many of his budget item requests. Hardy arrived early the day of that meeting at Raggio's office in downtown Reno to personally inform him that there were enough votes in the caucus to oust him. "He was not happy, of course," Hardy recalled. "As the caucus meeting commenced, he came into the room and listened to what people had to say. Some of us were going to vote for him to continue to be the leader. The vote went down, and the majority were for Senator McGinness."

When it came time to count votes, Senator Kieckhefer stayed loyal to Raggio and was joined by longtime, rural Senator Dean Rhoads. Raggio intervened, withdrawing from consideration because he did "not wish to subject Hardy, Rhoads, and Kieckhefer, who supported me, to further political pressure." In addition, Raggio, still protective of the party that was now leaving him behind, factored in the need for a unanimous vote as a show of Republican unity.

He was also aware that most of the caucus had made campaign commitments as to how they would deal with the extreme budget deficit facing them; commitments, he knew from experience, that would be impossible for them to keep. To avoid the daily frustration of watching the inevitable, Raggio requested that he not be reappointed as a member of the Senate Finance Committee.

Kieckhefer risked his fledgling political future by going against the majority in his first caucus meeting. "It was terrible. A tough way to start my legislative career," he recalled. Still, he never regretted doing what he thought was right, and rather than impeding his career, his constituents returned him to office time and again.

Raggio found it paradoxical that certain caucus members had been happy to take his endorsement and financial support in their 2009 races, knowing they would vote him out. "But even more ironic," he continued, "are ultraconservatives who constantly cite the U.S. Constitution and the Bill of Rights. I guess their view is that if you are a Republican and an elected official, you forego the right of free speech!"

He added that he had always been mindful that he was elected not just by Republican voters but by Democrats and independents, as well. "I did not take an oath to follow any party's platform."

> All I can say is that I did what I thought was right, and apparently, more people agreed with me than disagreed because Reid won by 40,000 votes. So, I guess I am with the majority of the people. The Republican Party simply put up a candidate who could not win.

The decision to end Raggio's tenure as Senate floor minority leader was met with a strong reaction on both sides. A former political adversary, retired Nevada Supreme Court Justice Bob Rose, said:

> There are always consequences if you go against another party member. Raggio has the courage of his convictions and expressed his opinion, an educated opinion. If something is really in the best interest of the State, he will do it regardless of the political consequences. He has always been that way.

On January 5, 2011, Senator Bill Raggio announced the end of his public service career. He had recently undergone back surgery, but more pertinent to his decision was a painful torn Achilles tendon, which significantly impeded his mobility. He had hoped to find a procedure to repair the tendon, but after consulting with one of the nation's foremost surgeons in that field, Raggio learned the probability of success at age eighty-four was too low to risk the surgery.

Jon Ralston, who had covered Raggio's career for decades, wrote in the *Las Vegas Sun* that, despite the health issues and Raggio being statutorily termed out in 2012, he was a proud man and would not want to hobble around the building, yet, "I think he would have put up with the pain if he were still leader."[96]

Sharron Angle released a statement:

> I warned voters in 2008 that Senator Raggio would vote
> to increase taxes again and then resign in the middle of
> his term to pave the way for an appointment rather than
> allowing the voters to elect his replacement. It's a
> premeditated endeavor to keep the 'good old boy'
> politics in play that the majority of Americans rallied
> against in the recent elections.[97]

Angle added she was unavailable for consideration as his replacement but urged her supporters to call on Washoe County commissioners to appoint a senator to vote against tax increases.

Upon resigning his seat in the Senate, Bill Raggio asked the Washoe County Commission to appoint "someone well-qualified, who shares my political values and who will commit to working with others and across party lines to do what is in the best interests of our communities and our State."

On January 18, 2011, his wish was granted when forty-six-year-old Greg Brower was appointed Raggio's replacement. An attorney like Raggio, Brower had served as a naval officer in the Pacific Fleet and at the Pentagon. He was elected to the Nevada Assembly in 1998 and served there until he was defeated in 2002 after redistricting—by Sharron Angle. After serving as counsel in the U.S. Justice Department and Government Printing Office, Brower was appointed by President George W. Bush as U.S. Attorney for the District of Nevada.

Like Raggio, Brower was very much his own person.

13

Partisan Gridlock

IN AUGUST 2011, BILL RAGGIO and his wife, Dale, traveled to New Orleans to attend the annual meeting of the American Legislative Exchange Council (ALEC), an influential organization whose mission was to form a public-private partnership of America's state legislators, business people, and federal officeholders to promote economic growth. One of the organization's most important functions was crafting model language for proposed pieces of legislation. In that regard, Raggio's expertise was highly valued. As one long-time ALEC member would say: "Bill has his fingerprints on every piece of legislation in the country. His advice reverberated far beyond the State of Nevada."[98]

As an early member of ALEC, Raggio served on the board of directors and was selected as the organization's national chairman in 1993. At that time, ALEC was veering toward becoming a vehicle of social, rather than fiscal, conservatism—a change that threatened its existence. Ron Scheberle, a fellow board member, was unequivocal in his praise for Raggio's leadership during the crisis, saying in 2009: "I would say, without hesitation, that ALEC would not be in existence today had it not been for Bill Raggio."

Senator Raggio, he added, understood that ALEC was at its best when it maintained a "free market, free enterprise, pro-business focus." Raggio, he said, guided the organization toward those goals of fiscal conservatism, managing to keep at arm's length those who wanted to use ALEC as a platform for their socially conservative agenda, pushing legislation against such issues as abortion, same-sex marriage, and gun control, while promoting prayer in schools and traditional family structures and values.

Bill Raggio certainly had his own opinions on these issues, but he was foremost a pragmatist. Scheberle said the private sector was vital in developing good and lasting fiscal policy. As such, Bill Raggio "was widely considered the most valuable member in the organization." [99]

In gratitude, ALEC created the William J. Raggio Excellence in Leadership and Outstanding Service Award, given to one of its members each year who best exemplified those qualities. Honored, Raggio always made a point of attending the presentation.

Yet, some within the organization resented Raggio's parliamentary ability to hinder their social agendas from achieving a national podium through ALEC and, while feigning respect, worked behind the scenes to discredit him. Their mood was inflamed in 1992 when Raggio insisted that ALEC present outgoing President George H. W. Bush with its prestigious Thomas Jefferson Freedom Award.

Raggio recalled, "There was some feeling, some resistance, in ALEC that Bush had not been conservative enough when he was President." During the economic recession in 1990, Bush signed budget reconciliation legislation that, among other things, raised taxes for top earners. Ultraconservatives felt he had given too much away in his compromise with the Democrats. But Raggio prevailed and personally presented the award to former President Bush at his office in Houston. The final straw for these ultraconservatives came in 2010 when Raggio endorsed Democratic Senator Harry Reid for reelection.

Throughout that week in New Orleans, Raggio, once sought out by attendees for his counsel or a photo-op, was now snubbed by all but a handful of his oldest friends. Few were willing to be seen with him publicly. The Nevada delegation steered a wide path. [100]

But what proved to be the most offensive and telling display of disapproval occurred when, despite staying in the hotel where the ceremony was being held, Raggio was not informed when the award bearing his name was to be presented—and so missed it. Ron Scheberle recalled that while it might have resulted from a simple mistake by the staff in scheduling him, it also could have been intentional: "I could see the pettiness."[101]

Bill Raggio did not doubt that it was anything other than a calculated and very public slap in the face and was deeply insulted—though not surprised—because he had seen this before.

Early in his days in ALEC, Raggio had befriended Republican Congressman Jack Kemp of New York. Kemp, a former Bush Administration Secretary of Health Education and Welfare, had, in 1981, fashioned a coalition in Congress that pushed through radical reductions in capital gains and income taxes. Some believed this legislation, often called the Kemp-Roth Tax Cut, ushered in America's most productive decade and world history's most remarkable peacetime economic expansion. Many in ALEC saw similarities between the philosophy and work ethic of Kemp and Raggio, admiring the way both came to the table prepared, were trustworthy, willing to compromise, and the fairness with which they treated others.

Kemp, who the GOP would select as vice presidential running mate with Bob Dole during the 1996 race, later said that party leadership did not fully endorse the ticket due to his stance on minority issues.[102] Kemp quoted poll numbers showing nearly 30 percent of Blacks identified themselves as conservatives on school prayer, school vouchers, and criminal justice. As such, he was chagrined his party did reach out to improve historically poor support from these voters.[103]

Despite his contributions, Kemp would end his career vilified by ultra-right extremists in his party for his endorsement of programs designed to reach minority voters and help the less fortunate move up the economic ladder. As with Raggio, Kemp became entirely unacceptable to this faction when he supported Senator John McCain in the 2008 Republican presidential primary election.

Jack Kemp passed away in 2009, two years before the ALEC meeting in New Orleans. *The Atlantic* said of him:

> At a time of ideological sectarianism, inflammatory
> talk, and intergroup division, Kemp symbolizes for
> many the hope for a more decent and humane

conservatism—a conservatism that leaves nobody out and nobody behind.[104]

This, too, mirrored Raggio's politics, as he had admonished others in his party to: "Stick to your values and keep your ears and eyes open to all sides. If you think you are wrong, don't be afraid to change, yet have some principles you believe in. That's why I'm a Republican."

*****

Raggio's departure from the state senate would be immediately significant because 2011 was a redistricting year. Unsurprisingly, that effort became so partisan and non-negotiable that the Legislature could not devise a plan acceptable to both sides. Latino representation in the recently awarded Fourth Congressional District was the primary source of contention.

When Republican Governor Brian Sandoval vetoed both redistricting maps passed by party-line votes and refused to call a special session to complete the process, Carson City District Judge Todd Russell appointed three special masters to complete redistricting. Raggio, now on the sidelines, had been intensely protective throughout his career of giving up to the other branches of government, even the slightest bit of authority granted to the Legislature by the Nevada Constitution, and was exasperated.

Critics viewed Republican intransigence on this issue as stemming from a fear of the political implications of Nevada's changing demographics. Since the previous census in 2000, Nevada had become the nation's fastest-growing state and one of the most urbanized and diverse. Specifically, nearly 75 percent of the population now resided in Clark County, and more than 45 percent of Nevadans were classified as non-White.

Nevada Democrats, assisted by U.S. Senate Majority Leader Harry Reid's extensive political organization, took advantage of these population trends to flip the State from Republican-leaning to Democrat-leaning. Instead of accepting this reality, and in the hope of a more favorable outcome, Nevada Republicans desperately turned to a strained interpretation of Section 2 of the Voting Rights Act, which might have gerrymandered Latinos into a single U.S. House district, marginalizing their influence in Nevada's other three U.S. House districts.

By forcing redistricting into the courts, Nevada Republicans miscalculated and ended up with a less favorable outcome than if they had accepted either of the Democrats' plans passed during the Legislative session. The special masters opted not to create a majority Latino House district, and Nevada Republicans had not even considered hiring a Latino outreach coordinator until after this court redistricting decision in 2011.[105]

As a plan to minimize minority votes, extremists in the Republican Party chose to scuttle a proposal by the State Chair for same-day registration. Yet, political analysts determined that same-day registration could have helped the GOP cut into the Democrats' 64,000-plus statewide edge. "Not since rabble-rousing Ron Paul delegates forced the shutdown of the 2008 State GOP convention," Jon Ralston wrote, "has the party been so exposed as a toxic warehouse of destructive, cannibalizing fools."[106]

When called back for his Senate Hall of Fame induction ceremony during this dysfunctional 2011 legislative session, Raggio told reporter Geoff Dornan with characteristically droll humor, "I'm looking like a genius for not being part of this."[107]

Bill Raggio died in Sydney, Australia, on February 24, 2012. In addition to her grief, Dale was suddenly faced with an enormous amount of Australian government red tape. Specific procedures had to be followed involving the death of a visitor from abroad, and officials told her it might be several weeks before her husband's body could be returned home.

When Senator Harry Reid heard about the death and the difficulty Dale was having with local authorities, he immediately contacted the State Department, followed by a personal phone call to the president of American Airlines. Raggio's casket was soon heading back to the United States.

A full military honor guard escort was waiting on the runway in Dallas as he was transferred to another plane bound for Reno. Ben Kieckhefer later postulated that while it was certainly generous of Reid to help, it may have been not so much a case of the GOP further distancing themselves from Raggio as that no one else had Reid's level of influence in government to be able to do that. Reid's biographer would later write that, despite his reputation as "polarizing and offensive," there were "countless stories of his private acts of kindness and compassion."[108]

Although Raggio reluctantly endorsed Reid against Sharron Angle in October 2010, making it clear that he disagreed with him on many issues, the two men had always maintained a respectful relationship. When contacted in 2021 to confirm his assistance getting Raggio home, Reid first said before any questions were asked: "If you are looking for me to say anything bad about Bill Raggio, it's not going to happen. He did great things for Nevada."

*****

Ron Paul returned to the Republican Party in 1996, having parted ways with the Libertarian Party on several platform stances. However, he was never again nominated and, after losing the 2008 primary election, again criticized Republicans, saying they were no different from the Democrats. He then refused to endorse John McCain, lending his support to a third-party candidate.

Paul declined to speak at the 2012 Republican National Convention after losing his bid to become presidential nominee. Convention planners had demanded that the Mitt Romney campaign vet his remarks and that he make an unqualified endorsement of Romney.

Many of Paul's supporters and delegates walked out of that convention in protest over the adoption of rules that reduced their delegate count and made it difficult for "non-establishment" candidates to win the party's nomination in the future. Supporters of Paul filed a lawsuit in U.S. District Court against the Republican National Committee and fifty-five state and territorial Republican

Party organizations. The suit claimed there had been "a systematic campaign of election fraud at state conventions," employing rigging of voting machines, ballot stuffing, and falsifying ballot totals to prevent votes for Paul from being counted.

But what should have most alarmed Republicans and Democrats alike was Paul's call for secession in the wake of the November 2012 election. Secession from the United States, Paul stated, "is a deeply American principle" and that if the possibility of secession is completely off the table, "there is nothing to stop the federal government from continuing to encroach on our liberties and no recourse for those who are sick and tired of it."[109]

Two years later, spurred by such rhetoric, southern Nevada rancher Cliven Bundy announced he did not recognize federal authority over the land after refusing to pay years of delinquent fees for grazing his cattle on public lands. The U.S. Bureau of Land Management began impounding his animals but soon faced a phalanx of armed militia whom Bundy had called upon to protect him. The authorities relented, and Bundy continued the willful trespass and nonpayment of fees.

He and his sons quickly became leading elements of the anti-government movement in the West. Two years later, the brothers, demanding that the federal government turn over all public lands to the states for private development, led an armed occupation of the Malheur National Wildlife Refuge in Oregon, resulting in the shooting death by authorities of one of their supporters. After nearly two years in pretrial detention, the brothers went free due to a legal technicality and faced no further consequences.

Nevada U.S. Senator Dean Heller validated Bundy's methods by calling him and his followers "patriots." On the other side of the aisle, Harry Reid called them "domestic terrorists" and warned prophetically: "We can't have an American people that violate the law and then just walk away from it. So, it's not over."

Nationalist groups, such as Posse Comitatus and the Aryan Nations, saw militia and patriot movements as a form of white resistance against what they perceived as a liberal and multiculturalist government. Their worst nightmare had come true years earlier, in

January 2009, when U.S. Senator Barack Obama of Illinois became the 44th President of the United States.

*****

In 2014, the Republican Party gained complete control of the Nevada State government for the first time since 1929, sweeping to victory in the Assembly and the Senate and retaining control of the governor's mansion. The Nevada State Senate chose Las Vegas attorney Michael Roberson as its floor leader.

Assemblyman Ira Hansen was the Republican candidate for Speaker of the Assembly.[110] Like the Bundys and their followers, Hansen was a staunch advocate of the federal government transferring control of land in Nevada to the State. He sponsored a Senate joint resolution urging Congress to transfer the title of some public lands to the State, with a requirement that the federal government share receipts from commercial activity on the land with the State and counties in which the activities are performed.

Hansen had become a predominant and articulate voice of the ultra-right wing of the Republican Party in Nevada. In 1967, his father, Daniel, had started the Independent American Party of Nevada, whose platform emphasized American nationalism, Christian ethics, and the traditionalist conservatism of the Republican "Old Right" that had opposed President Franklin Roosevelt's New Deal. In the 1968 election, Daniel Hansen was Nevada campaign manager for the American Independent Party presidential candidate, segregationist Alabama Governor George Wallace.

Following the announcement of Ira Hansen's impending selection as Speaker, journalist Dennis Myers, whose liberal political views put him at odds with Hansen's and with whom he had worked at the *Sparks Tribune,* conducted an extensive search of an estimated 800 columns Hansen wrote for that paper from 1994 through 2010.

Among the ideas Myers found that Hansen had written was that the 1995 Oklahoma City right-wing domestic terrorist bombing, which killed 168 people, had been secretly orchestrated by the Clinton Administration; that women do not belong in the United States Armed

123

Forces, except for limited assignments; that gay men were disproportionally prone to pedophilia; and that Latinos committed a "grossly disproportionate" number of crimes. According to Myers, Hansen displayed a Confederate flag on the wall of his office. [111] Hansen said Meyers cherry-picked those stories out of the hundreds he had written for maximum shock value.

Myers's story in the *Reno News & Review* was picked up nationally and drew widespread attention and considerable approbation. Upon its release, Hansen apologized in an open letter on the press page of his website, saying:

> As a columnist, I was encouraged to write provocatively, but over the last 20 years, I have learned that there is a line between being provocative and being offensive. There were times when I crossed that line. My intention was not to offend, and I sincerely apologize for any offense I have caused.

Despite Hansen's apology, these disclosures resulted in Republican Governor Brian Sandoval and other party leaders distancing themselves from him and the negative image he brought to the party, pressuring him to step down from consideration as speaker.

In announcing that, Hansen stated this had been a carefully orchestrated attack to remove a conservative Republican from a major leadership role in State government and that "the deliberate character assassination and the politics of personal destruction have totally distorted my views and record." The information had not surfaced over his two terms as an Assemblyman, but did now because "the powers that be are planning a massive tax increase and I stood in the way as Speaker…that this smear campaign occurred."

Assemblyman Pat Hickey, who had been minority party leader for the previous two sessions, believed he would be the speaker. However, ultraconservatives in the Assembly were powerful enough to block his selection, considering Hickey too moderate. With Ira Hansen out of the race, they selected John Hambrick from Clark County.

During the campaign that year, Hickey adopted the Reagan-era approach of "principled pragmatism" rather than "party purity," a political style that, he said, had worked so effectively for Senator Bill Raggio. He saw the Republican victory in 2014 not as a Red Wave but "a Blue puddle" because Democratic voters, now taking election-year victories for granted, had failed to show up in significant enough numbers at the polls. If the Nevada GOP did not end the infighting and exclusion of other points of view, Hickey said, Democrats would return to stay. His words turned out to be prophetic, beginning with the next election.

*****

Despite this inauspicious start to the 2015 session, it would, surprisingly, become a model of traditional negotiation.

Necessary votes were obtained through bargaining, led by hugely popular Republican Governor Brian Sandoval. To win support from more conservative Republicans, Sandoval linked the tax increase to other education reforms, including a robust parents' choice measure providing funds to families with children in private schools. Passage of the bill required a two-thirds majority in the Assembly, achieved after Sandoval's staff engaged in a last-minute, high-pressure lobbying effort over the objections of ten anti-tax conservatives led by Senator Hansen.

"After Raggio left, the power structure did not change," Hansen said. "Sandoval got elected in his first session by promising to be conservative about taxes, school choice, etc. But the minute he won the election, he did exactly what gaming wanted."

Moderate Republicans, like State Senator Ben Kieckhefer, recalled that session more positively. Sandoval, he said, was so popular that when he ran for reelection, Democrats did not bother supporting a viable opponent:

> The 2015 session was a textbook of legislative and government mastery. There was a great deal of

pushback, but decisions had to be made. It was a master class in legislative leadership.

14

Legislative Terrorists

On June 10, 2014, Republican U.S. House Majority Leader Eric Cantor was defeated by Tea Party candidate Dave Brat in Virginia's Republican Primary election, described by the Los Angeles Times as "one of the greatest political upsets of modern times."[112] Cantor's predecessor, Ohio Republican John Boehner, possessed a working-class background, openness, integrity, and willingness to negotiate that was reminiscent of Bill Raggio's political style, or as one newspaper wrote, "he perfected the art of disagreeing without being disagreeable."[113].

Boehner came to power on the momentum of the 2010 Tea Party wave but soon clashed with those in the movement over taxes, the federal debt limit, and Obamacare. He and President Obama worked hard to close a deal involving sweeping fiscal matters but could not agree on a final plan. Boehner's persona alienated ultra-conservative Republicans who demanded more vigorous attacks on the president. Later he would write, "I took the Speaker's gavel in 2011, two years into the Obama presidency... every second of every day since Barack Obama became president, I was fighting one batshit idea after another."[114]

In a time of strident confrontation on talk radio or cable TV, Boehner's easygoing style did not fit. He despised the cruelty of modern politics and the angry, unbending tenor in his party. "It doesn't cost anything to be nice," was his constant refrain. It did not help that he had relished working with Democratic Senator Ted Kennedy, whom he publicly called "a great man and a great legislator," or his vocal disdain for Texas Republican Senator Ted Cruz, whom he described as the ringleader of the Tea Party movement.

Boehner added: "What they're really interested in is chaos.... They want to throw sand in the gears of the hated federal government until it fails, and they've finally proved that it's beyond saving." And, "Every time they vote down a bill, they get another invitation to go on Fox News or talk radio," he said. "It's a narcissistic—and dangerous—feedback loop."[115]

He advised those who genuinely wished to fix government "to send people there to represent you and who actually want to get things done, instead of hucksters making pie-in-the-sky promises or legislative terrorists just looking to go to Washington and blow everything up."

Echoing Raggio's complaint that these radical conservatives who worshiped Ronald Reagan were far beyond Reagan's level of conservativism, Boehner said he believed that Ronald Reagan would be considered too moderate a conservative to get elected in today's Republican Party. And, like Raggio, who had been stripped of his party leadership role four years earlier in Nevada, Boehner was effectively cast out as House speaker in 2015 in a revolt by the Tea Party elements within the GOP and subsequently resigned from Congress.

With each passing session, partisan feuding and obstructionism increased, often grinding the process to a halt. The mood of the Nevada State Legislature reflected this growing political divisiveness. Two months after Bill Raggio died in 2012, a pair of the nation's most respected scholars of American politics would write:

> The GOP has become an insurgent outlier in American politics. It is ideologically extreme; scornful of compromise; unmoved by conventional understanding of facts, evidence, and science; and dismissive of the legitimacy of its political opposition...all but declaring war on the government.[116]

*****

In March 2013, Republican National Committee Chairman Reince Priebus provided an in-depth report on his party's failures in the 2012 election, including candidate Mitt Romney's loss to incumbent President Obama. He called on the party to reinvent itself and proposed reforms, including a $10 million marketing campaign to reach women, minorities, and gays and immigration reform.[117]

Since the time of pro-immigration Ronald Reagan, Republicans have been divided on how to confront illegal immigration. The Republican establishment generally supported a platform that allowed for the entry of migrant workers and a path to citizenship for undocumented immigrants. Nativist-leaning Republicans focused on securing the southern border and deporting illegal immigrants. In 2006, President George W. Bush and the Republican-led Senate passed comprehensive immigration reform that would eventually allow millions of illegal immigrants to become citizens. However, the House, also controlled by Republicans, did not advance the measure.

As the 2016 National Republican primary approached, millionaire property developer and reality show television celebrity Donald Trump possessed one distinct advantage over others seeking his party's presidential nomination—his willingness to parrot often false conservative media rhetoric.

For years, he had a weekly time slot on *Fox News's Fox & Friends*, gaining notoriety for amplifying claims that President Barack Obama was an illegitimate president because he was not born a citizen of the United States. He would comment on current events weekly and use his Twitter and Facebook accounts to malign Obama. He eventually transitioned from unconcealed "birtherism" to insinuating that Obama was a radical Islamic plant. After Obama won reelection, Trump's social media moved into such extreme exaggerations and lies that the Republican Party establishment tried to keep him at arm's length.

A year earlier, Bill Raggio had observed: "It is obvious this blind anger that right-wing radicals exhibit is fanned and fumed by right-wing media," which he had repeatedly denounced as a "form of entertainment that these people take as gospel."

A federal court judge would later confirm Raggio's observation. In September 2020, Fox News's most vocal and influential Trump devotee, Tucker Carlson, regularly engaged in unfounded claims, resulting in a defamation lawsuit against him and Fox. Network attorneys argued that no "reasonable viewer" takes Carlson seriously. U.S. District Judge Mary Kay Vyskocil agreed with Fox's premise. "Given Mr. Carlson's reputation, any reasonable viewer arrives with an appropriate amount of skepticism about the statements he makes," Vyskocil ruled. She added that the general tenor of the show should inform a viewer that Carlson is "not stating actual facts" about the topics he discusses and is instead engaging in "exaggeration and non-literal commentary." [118]

But, unlike Ira Hansen a few years earlier, who had drawn national attention for writing provocatively but learned the line between provocative and offensive, Carlson would become deliberately more offensive. In April 2023, Fox News agreed to pay Dominion Voting Systems $787 million to avert a trial in the company's lawsuit that would have exposed how Fox, particularly Tucker Carlson, promoted knowing lies about the 2020 presidential election. The network subsequently fired Carlson.

Donald Trump, the GOP candidate in 2016, did just the opposite of Priebus's 2013 recommendations, instead appealing to voters who held exclusionary, nationalist, White supremacist, and anti-immigrant views. Among his most popular campaign promises was to build a wall along the country's southern border. Within that base, Trump found he was able to abandon traditional Republican issues, like trade and government spending, in favor of a nationalist message, and in doing so, won the election with an Electoral College victory of 304-227, though losing the popular vote by 2.9 million.

Months before, filmmaker and liberal icon Michael Moore predicted Trump's victory. Moore pointed out it would not matter that the left had seemingly won "the culture wars," with a majority of Americans now taking a liberal position on just about every polling question posed to them: equal pay for women, gay and lesbian marriage, legalized abortion, effective environmental laws, and gun control.[119] What mattered, he said, was that working-class, predominantly white voters overwhelmingly felt resentment toward the news and film industries, centered in New York City and Hollywood, who, in the minds of those voters, were intellectually smug and mockingly disdainful of their conservative values.

Journalist David Brooks, long an eloquent voice of the conservativism of William F. Buckley and Ronald Reagan, would agree, saying that by 2016:

> America was fragmenting. Whole regions had been left behind, and many elite institutions had shifted sharply left and driven conservatives from their ranks. Social media had instigated a brutal war of all against all, social trust was cratering, and the leadership class was growing more isolated, imperious, and condescending.[120]

Presenting facts to disprove Trump's often-dubious claims along the campaign trail would not matter. Because the biggest problem the Democrats had, Moore wrote, was not Donald Trump—it was Hillary Clinton.

Widely unpopular—with nearly 70 percent of all voters believing her to be untrustworthy—Clinton represented, Moore said, the old politics of not believing in anything other than what could get her elected. Somewhat surprisingly, young women were among her biggest detractors. The enthusiasm they felt for Barack Obama and Bernie Sanders in the primaries was not there. Countless young people who could not vote for Trump simply did not go to the polls. Trump voters, on the other hand, were motivated.

The Trump campaign focused much of its attention on traditionally Democratic states in the Rustbelt of the upper Great Lakes. There, Trump would hammer home the Clintons' support of the North American Free Trade Agreement and Trans-Pacific Partnership pact that damaged the economies in the industrial states of the Upper Midwest.

This was, Moore said, music to the ears of what was once called the middle class, now angry, embittered working (and nonworking) people who were lied to by the trickle-down of Reagan and abandoned by Democrats. "They did not have to agree with Trump or condone his behavior," Moore said, "because he was their messenger that a broken political system had left them behind—and they did not like it one bit."

Moore explained that all Trump needed to do to win was carry the swath of traditional Red States from Idaho to Georgia, unalterably repulsed by Hillary Clinton, and then the 64 electoral votes from four traditionally Democrat-controlled Rust Belt states. And that is precisely what happened.

Ira Hansen would talk of Trump's 2016 victory, saying the Republican Party was then still controlled by elitists who endorsed Jeb Bush in the primary election. "Yet, within the party apparatus, lo and behold, this 'crazy guy' named Donald Trump shows up:"

> People were so hungry for a non-politician politician that, even though he was an adulterer who did all these bad things and a billionaire businessman, we loved him. What happened to the Republican establishment was backlash, and Donald Trump was a great president.

Some political historians would later argue that Donald Trump was not so much an outlier as a manifestation of the attack-mode political groundwork laid down twenty-five years earlier by Newt Gingrich—and so was now a perfect candidate for the modern Republican Party.[121]

*****

Over the preceding decade, Nevada had undergone a political transformation from a reliable Republican outpost to an emerging Democratic stronghold. During the 2018 midterm election, Nevada GOP candidates Senator Dean Heller, Adam Laxalt, and lieutenant governor hopeful Senator Michael Roberson planned to coat-tail on President Trump's 2016 election success by employing anti-immigration fear tactics. Although they each won by landslides in the sparsely populated counties, they alienated urban residents and brought out minority voters like never before. The three lost their races by significant margins, helping turn the State bluer.

As Republicans dug in on such issues, and the demographics in Clark County became more Democratic, they would lose a majority in both State legislative houses. By 2018, the governorship went to a Democrat for the first time in twenty years. Over the same decade, Nevada added 165,000 more registered Democrats. By 2020, out of the 1.5 million registered voters in the State, approximately 630,000 were Democrat, 505,000 Republican, and 270,000 were not affiliated with a political party.[122]

The most notable change had been in Washoe County, a place long considered a GOP stronghold, part of which Raggio represented for thirty-eight years in the State Senate. An influx of California transplants, mainly due to a tech industry boom, had drawn college-educated voters who tend toward progressive rather than conservative values. But not all the California transplants were Democrats. Chris Wicker, the former Washoe County Democratic chairman, said the influx from California is a "mixed bag" politically:

> Many people are coming to northern Nevada to avoid taxes or their company is moving here. They are not necessarily naturally Democrats just because they came from California. Many young people register as non-partisan but show up at progressive groups' events. [123]

For decades, the key to Republican success in Nevada statewide elections was to win all the conservative rural counties and get enough votes in Washoe County to offset heavily Democratic Clark County. In 2008, President Obama became the first Democrat since Lyndon Johnson in 1964 to carry Washoe County.

Most credited Harry Reid with the Democratic Party's success in the State. Seeing the future clearly, Reid had placated organized labor and worked with groups registering young and Latino voters. Ira Hansen explained how Reid was able to channel money from the unions and casinos:

Because he controls the finances and chooses the candidates that he and the unions want, he runs the Nevada Legislature. Raggio was never able to get to a point where *all* the money channeled through him, though he exercised a good deal of power through his Senate Republican Leadership Caucus Fund.

As Senate majority leader, Raggio always protected gaming and higher education above all others, Hansen said, but despite that, he respected Raggio "more so now than when I was a talk radio person, or as part of the Tea Party." The reason for that, Hansen said: "After being in this [Legislature] building, I now understand how difficult the process can be… because you have to be a pragmatist. That is where Raggio excelled. He respected the institution." An example of such respect, Hansen said, was that despite Senator Raggio having been a long-time target of public criticism by Hansen, "he freely shared his half a century of institutional knowledge with me as a freshman senator."

Ben Kieckhefer pointed out that long periods of gridlock in Congress over the last forty years have made it difficult to achieve long-term public policy. So, policy decisions at the state level are driven by national groups, and both major national parties now draw the state districting maps—once the province of state legislatures. The breakdown of the checks-and-balances system, particularly the loss of independence by state legislatures, was becoming a problem that benefited authoritarians and others who shunned cooperation with those who disagreed.

Many, like Warren Hardy, saw more and more legislative power slipping away, saying that over the last twenty years, the Legislative Branch, both nationally and in the states, has become the political arm of the Executive Branch:

Beginning with Bill Clinton and becoming much worse once Donald Trump took office, the Legislature has been moving away from the checks and balances it was intended to safeguard against authoritarian rule. It is now delegated to passing the governor's or president's agenda.

Senator Raggio had been vigilant about not giving up legislative jurisdiction to either the judiciary or the executive branches and empowered the concept of legislative prerogative by pushing the idea that anything not mentioned in the Nevada Constitution was deemed the Legislature's responsibility. The Legislature's primary source of power was that it held the state government's purse strings, though Hardy had seen that diminish, as well:

> I recall going into Governor Guinn's and later Governor Gibbons's office with Raggio, who would sit down and tell them which items in the governor's executive budget proposal were going to be acceptable to the Legislature and which were not. That would be impossible today.

*****

As Tea Party influence surged, establishment Republicans sought the middle ground, but President Trump's rigid demand for personal loyalty made that impossible. While many GOP legislators across the country, at every level of government, enthusiastically agreed with Trump's authoritarian, bombastic, messianic style, almost all those who did not feared alienating him. This became fertile ground for giving a national voice to previously marginal elements espousing antigovernment conspiracy theories.

In August 2017, a White supremacist rally called Unite the Right in Charlottesville, Virginia, occurred amidst backlash generated by the removal of Confederate monuments throughout the South by local governments following the Charleston, South Carolina, church shooting in 2015, in which a teenage White supremacist shot and killed nine black church members, including the minister (a state senator), and wounded several others.

Among the participants at the Charlottesville rally were self-identified neo-fascists, White nationalists, Klansmen, and various right-wing militias. Some groups chanted racist and anti-Semitic slogans while carrying Nazi and neo-Nazi symbols, Confederate battle flags, and guns. The organizers' short-term goal was to prevent the proposed removal of the statue honoring a Confederate general from a local park. While the organizers intended for the rally to unite far-right groups to play a more prominent role in American politics, the backlash and resultant infighting caused a decline in the movement.

In May 2020, the Black Lives Matter movement returned to the forefront of national and international attention during global protests following the digitally recorded public killing of a black man by a white Minneapolis police officer. It would grow into one of the largest protest movements in U.S. history, with an estimated 15 million to 26 million participating worldwide. The rise in urban violence related to some Black Lives Matter protests provided renewed momentum for Unite the Right extremist groups. During President Trump's final weeks in office, these radical-right groups found common cause around his claim that the 2020 presidential election had been stolen.

15

Ballot Integrity

NEVADA'S DEMOGRAPHIC MATHEMATICS for the future does not favor the Republican Party. Longtime Nevada political observer Fred Lokken believed Nevada had joined West Coast states like Washington, Oregon, and Hawaii, where Democrats have been in power for some time and a growing population of Asians and Pacific Islanders are adding to the changing demographic. Yet, Nevada's GOP made almost no effort to tap into this new pool of voters. Instead, the party took a turn even further right, embracing hardline policies of nationalism and exclusion, and later President Trump's anti-immigration platform, making the party too conservative for many Republicans. [124]

In ramping up its push to win Nevada back in 2020, the party focused on an economic message aimed at nonpartisan and moderate voters. It argued that Democrats were too extreme for most voters. "If these 2020 Democrats honestly believe their socialist agenda is a winning message in Nevada, they are going to be severely disappointed," said Nevada GOP Chairman Michael McDonald. It would prove to be a crucial decision for the state GOP because if they were wrong, Democrats would oversee redistricting in 2021, further bad news in their efforts to rebound.

During the 2020 presidential election, former U.S. senator and vice president Joe Biden flipped Arizona, Georgia, Michigan, Pennsylvania, and Wisconsin to win the Electoral College vote. Every other state held to form. The final tally was 306-232, with Biden winning the popular vote by seven million. Voter turnout in 2020 was 66.7 percent of the voting-eligible population—the highest in 120 years.[125]

Well before the election, President Trump suggested the election would be rigged in Biden's favor. And, in the aftermath of his loss, he continued asserting that he had been the victim of widespread voter fraud.

The modern myth of pervasive voter fraud first took shape in 1986, proving to be an effective tool for the national Republican Party at a time when Republicans recognized that their far-right-leaning policies were becoming increasingly unpopular with a majority of voters. That year marked President Ronald Reagan's sixth in office, and his approved budget cuts did not favor poorer Americans. His attempt to weaken Social Security just before the midterm elections and defend vulnerable senators elected on his coattails in 1980 forced Republicans to face the grim reality. Either change their policies or change the composition of their electorate.

They chose to launch a "ballot integrity" campaign to prevent voter fraud, claiming Democratic-leaning election officials were allowing dead or fictitious people to vote. Republican officials sent mail to registered voters in heavily Democratic areas of Louisiana, Indiana, and Missouri. If the mail returned as undeliverable, that person was purged from the voter rolls. Democrats sued, and the subsequent discovery process turned up a memo between Republican National Committee officials explaining the purpose behind the program: "If it's a close race, which I'm assuming it is, this could keep the Black vote down considerably."[126]

In 1992, after Bill Clinton was elected president, Democrats passed the Motor Voter Act, making registering to vote easier. Republicans howled that Democrats were packing elections. Representative Newt Gingrich, then the House minority whip, angrily predicted that illegal immigrants would now register to vote, and a wave of 300,000 illegal voters would soon bolster the Democrats.

In 1998, the Republican-dominated Florida legislature enacted reforms to prevent voter fraud by outsourcing voter list maintenance to a private company that purged voter rolls. A later study by the U.S. Commission on Civil Rights described an "extraordinarily high and inexcusable level of disenfranchisement" of Black voters in Florida. In addition, eliminating key voting places and limiting the number of available voting machines suppressed the vote by making wait times discouragingly long, contributing to Republican George W. Bush gaining the White House.

By 2000, the claim of widespread voter fraud had become a political staple among the right-wing of the Republican Party. As that theory echoed into familiarity, more and more Republicans came to treat every Democratic victory, regardless of the facts, as illegitimate.

In 2013, the U.S. Supreme Court, by a 5-4 vote, allowed nine states, mainly in the South, to change their election laws without advance federal approval, removing the heart of the Voting Rights Act of 1965. The majority opinion concluded that racial minorities no longer faced barriers to voting in those states with a history of discrimination.

Critics used President Obama's election as the nation's first black president as evidence that this law was no longer needed to ensure fair elections. Chief Justice Roberts wrote that Congress remained free to try to impose federal oversight on states where voting rights were at risk but must do so based on contemporary data.

*****

President Trump declared that Biden had won because of widespread voter fraud. He pressed forward with dozens of legal challenges, losing them all due to lack of evidence, before pressuring state election officials to "find" the votes he needed to win.[127]

When this failed, he pressured state officials to create false slates of electors who chose him rather than Biden. He then sought to have the Department of Justice validate that slate by charging the election was fraudulent. No one at the Department of Justice saw evidence of such fraud, so they refused. When the president attempted to install a loyalist to head the department, leaders within that organization threatened wholesale resignations.

Next, the President, along with his attorney John Eastman, hatched a plan to pressure Vice President Mike Pence, who was

139

overseeing the electoral ballot count, to tally only the competing illegitimate ballots submitted by his loyalists, giving him the victory. Eastman later admitted that this plan was illegal.

When Pence refused to participate in the scheme, Trump went to his final card—calling upon his extremist base to stop the congressional process. On December 19, 2020, with all his legal challenges exhausted and the electoral votes scheduled to be officially counted and filed on January 6, President Trump took to social media, urging his supporters to come to Washington, D.C., on that day, falsely claiming that it was statistically impossible for him to have lost the election, and commanding them: "Be there, will be wild."

The right-wing militias he had courted since the Charlottesville Unite the Right rally of August 2017 heard the message. They interpreted his tweet as an order to come to Washington to keep him in office, with violence if necessary, and planned accordingly. When the vice president remained unintimidated, Trump whipped up the crowd against Pence and ordered them to "fight like hell" for him, then sent them toward the Capitol, where the rare occurrence of both houses of Congress and the vice president were meeting.

Thus, on the afternoon of January 6, 2021, precisely ten years having elapsed since Bill Raggio resigned in despair from the Nevada State Senate after warning of the dire long-term consequences of turning the Republican Party over to far-right radicals, the United States Capitol Building was violently attacked by hundreds of President Trump's supporters.

Those who invaded the Capitol occupied and vandalized the building for several hours, killing and injuring Congressional Police officers trying to stop them and hunting for those they considered enemies of America, particularly Vice President Pence, demanding his execution by hanging for treason.

The President delayed calling in National Guard troops to protect the Capitol, and, in the end, five people died as a result of the attack, and 138 police officers and reinforcements were injured. Other officers who had battled the attackers later died due to the psychological trauma. It had all the earmarks of an insurrection to overthrow the constitutionally elected government. Yet, following the storming of the Capitol, a survey conducted by the American Enterprise Institute found that 40 percent of Republicans and 60 percent of White evangelical Republicans agreed that political violence is justifiable and could be necessary.[128]

In Nevada, Hansen would later say of the January 6 attack on Congress that Trump might have "helped exacerbate the problem," but that such inflammatory language had been used by Democrats, like [California Congresswoman] Maxine Waters, encouraging violent actions. More of a factor, Hansen said, was that the mainstream media press unfairly treated President Trump. "Trump would have some level of culpability for what he said, but it is like trying to extrapolate that he's maybe guilty of 5 percent but gets the blame for the other 95 percent."

As far as "stop the steal," Hansen said that, while he is not a conspiracy theorist, the history of elections in the United States is rife with examples of rigging to some degree. As recently as the 1960s, the John Kennedy and Lyndon Johnson campaigns were well-known for manipulating ballot counts.

After the January insurrection, some corporations announced they would no longer donate to Republicans who had voted to challenge the certified electoral votes, while others declared a moratorium on all political spending. Vice President Pence denounced the president. Republican Senate Majority Leader Mitch McConnell stood on the floor of the Senate just after the January 6 attack and put Trump at the center of the insurrection, saying, "The mob was fed lies. They were provoked by the President and other powerful people."[129] However, as time went on, and Trump retained his power over Republican politics, McConnell, and most in the party, did not dare to continue resistance.

Former Republican Speaker of the House John Boehner focused on themes that the late Bill Raggio had so prophetically warned about ten years earlier. "The legislative terrorism that I'd witnessed as a speaker had now encouraged actual terrorism." As for the President's accusations that bureaucrats within his Executive Branch agencies, such as the Justice Department and CIA, were part of a massive conspiracy against America to deprive them of a fair election, Boehner wrote:

> There is something very destructive—not to mention delusional—about the notion that there is some plot deep within the nation's capital—in the FBI, in the federal courts, in the intelligence community—to undermine democratically elected officials.[130]

In 2021, the House of Representatives impeached Trump for a second time in a year, charging him with, among other items, "incitement of insurrection." The Senate failed to convict along party lines, as they had during a trial earlier in the year. Eight Republican Senators broke ranks and voted to convict. Senator Mitch McConnell, who had unequivocally blamed Trump for insurrection on January 6, shied away when the time came to hold the president accountable.

Yet, some blamed Trump for not going further in his effort to seize power on January 6. Nevada's Cliven Bundy, who had threatened violence against federal officers in an armed standoff near his family's southern Nevada ranch in 2014, was disappointed in the President for not doing more:

> Today, President Trump had hundreds of thousands of people, and he pointed the way—pointed towards Congress and nodded his head to get the job done. We the People did clear the chambers of Congress. Trump blew his trumpet of retreat as the sun goes down.[131]

*****

Claims of voter fraud continued throughout 2021, but the evidence was lacking in every case. Such claims were not new, especially in Nevada.

When Sharron Angle narrowly lost the Republican primary for U.S. Congress in Nevada's Second Congressional District to Dean Heller in 2006, she immediately called for a new election because some poll workers in Washoe County, where she was the strongest, showed up late for work, or did not show up at all. A district court judge denied her appeal for a new election.[132]

In 2010, after losing her U.S. Senate race to Harry Reid, Angle claimed the election had been rigged.[133] She returned to statewide politics in 2016, unsuccessfully challenging fellow Republican Joe Heck for a congressional seat, promising to scour the country for voter fraud.

Nevada Secretary of State Barbara Cegavske, a Republican, stood firm when members of her party sought to overturn Nevada's 2020 presidential election results. On December 14, six weeks after Election Day, she discharged her constitutional duty by presiding over a video conference call where the State's six electors cast votes for Joe Biden. Outside the State Capitol building, six self-declared electors, with no legal authority, declared President Trump the unanimous victor.

Later evidence would indicate that those Nevada Republicans had pressured her to join them. Cegavske declined to comment on that in detail but did acknowledge that during the time President Trump was calling other secretaries of state, such as Georgia's Brad Raffensperger, to "find" votes that would allow him to win, she had declined to take a phone call from Air Force One: "I just stuck up for the law because I thought that was the right thing to do, which it was."

Cegavske said that threatening behavior from conspiracy-minded, far-right radicals had driven at least eight county election officials to leave office voluntarily. She had also been subject to that kind of intimidation, which included publishing her address on social media accompanied by drone footage of her home, raising concern for her family's safety, including grandchildren and pets.

In early March 2021, the Nevada Republican Party leadership provided her office with four boxes claiming to contain 122,000 reports of irregularities in the election. Cegavske's office reviewed the contents of the boxes and, after investigation, issued a verdict in a thirteen-page report concluding that there was no evidence of anything approaching widespread fraud.

The four boxes, she said, contained names that her office had already flagged—instances in which someone with Alzheimer's appeared to have voted twice, for example, or a "Jr." or "Sr." was left off similar names. Yet, after the 160-plus hours that her staff spent combing through the contents: "There was never ever enough to reject any election that had happened based on what we had."[134] "There's always fraud in elections," she later said. "There are always people that tried to do bad things, but it's a very, very small amount, and it never could amount to the races being turned over."

During her investigation, the Nevada Republican Party Central Committee voted 126-112 to censure Cegavske, claiming she had failed to "put the reliability of our elections in Nevada in question." The censure, later amended before a vote, initially banned Cegavske from party endorsements or resources for "the intense dishonor her failures brought upon the Nevada Republican Party." She did not give in to this pressure and pushed back against the premise of the censure in a public statement:

> My job is to carry out the duties of my office as enacted by the Nevada Legislature, not carry water for the State GOP or put my thumb on the scale of democracy. Unfortunately, members of my party continue to believe the 2020 general election was wrought with fraud—and that, somehow, I had a part in it—despite a complete lack of evidence to support that belief.
>
> Regardless of the censure vote today by the Nevada Republican Party Central Committee, I will continue in my efforts to oversee secure elections in Nevada and to restore confidence in our elections, confidence which has been destroyed by those falsely claiming the 2020 general election produced widespread fraud.[135]

Ten years before, as a Nevada state senator and veteran member of the Republican caucus, Cegavske had taken the no-tax pledge and embraced the emerging Tea Party. During several sessions, she had been at odds with Senator Raggio for not being conservative enough, especially regarding taxation and cutting funds for education and social services.

Raggio's repeated warnings about the dangers from ultraconservative elements and his dramatic stand against blind partisanship with his 2010 endorsement of Democratic Senator Harry Reid over Tea Party challenger Sharron Angle had goaded Cegavske to lead the effort to remove him from his longtime leadership role in the Senate Republican caucus. Far-right Republicans in Nevada had a no more steadfast a soldier in their cause over the last twenty years than Barbara Cegavske. As such, it now seemed no one was immune from the rising level of paranoia taking over the GOP.

After the election, Las Vegas-based political reporter Steve Sebelius wrote how Republican-led voter disenfranchisement had actually worked against the party, especially in their resistance to mail-in ballots. He quoted Republican candidate Drew Johnson, who had lost his run for a seat on the Clark County Commission by just a few hundred votes, saying that while there was no voter fraud involved—fraud did play a role.

"Many of these Republicans didn't vote because people in our party's leadership, other GOP candidates, and respected grassroots conservative activists led them to believe the election was rigged," Johnson said. The party told potential Republican voters that voting by mail wasn't secure, leading them to opt out of receiving mail ballots. As a result, these people had no ballot to drop off when terrible weather and long lines deterred them from voting in person on Election Day. "The threat of fraud caused us, as Republicans, to rig the election against ourselves," Johnson concluded. [136]

Journalist Jeff Greenfield wrote that one of the striking aspects of our current politics is "the growing disdain of some in the Republican universe for the whole idea that majorities get to govern." Rather than trying to broaden their share of the vote, Republicans prefer to offer "voter integrity" proposals driven by the unspoken conviction that "the wrong people are voting." [137]

*****

In October 2020, Greg Brower, who had been appointed to replace Bill Raggio in the State Senate in 2011, signed a letter, along with nineteen other Republican-appointed former U.S. Attorneys, calling President Donald Trump "a threat to the rule of law in our country" and endorsed Joe Biden.

During an interview the following year, Brower said:

> I do not see any organized way the Republicans can turn things around at this point because there is no willingness on the part of Republican elected officials to become involved. All I really see is fear and cowardice among Republicans who are afraid to go against Trump, afraid to go against those who support Trump, and afraid to speak up for what is right.

The GOP's election apparatus at every level was, he said, "just dominated by the Trump loyalists."

Warren Hardy added he was highly pessimistic about the possibility of changing this "because the far left and the far right have taken over their parties' primary process, and without open primaries, it will be virtually impossible to break that pattern. Both parties would object to open primaries in Nevada." [138]

After Senator John McCain died, Brower said, there did not seem to be among current Republican officeholders any who dared to buck Trump's influence over the party. "They've become spineless in their fear of losing a primary."

What made it worse, Brower said, was that these fearful politicians know better. He had spent years in Washington, D.C. inner circles, including stints with the FBI as Deputy General Counsel and later the Agency's Assistant Director of the Office of Congressional Affairs, and was appalled by the shameless hypocrisy:

> The reality is that behind closed doors, in private, they talk about how unqualified and unfit Trump is for

office. Yet, in public, they say something different. That's the most disappointing thing: that people who used to be honorable public servants and know better are willing to pretend because they do not want to get punitively primaried.

The threat of unfounded smears by the former president and his apologists against highly respected government and military leaders continues to challenge the courage of Americans to stand up for the Constitution in ways that have not been seen since the McCarthy era of the 1950s.

EPILOGUE

Some would argue that most people underestimated the influence and power of the modern American political right, which is comprised of populist, nativist, collectivist, authoritarian, and conspiracy-minded movements. They also overestimated the more libertarian impact of William F. Buckley's limited government, free trade, and free-market intellectual conservatism and Ronald Reagan's pro-immigration and optimistic outlook.[139]

Peter Wehner, who served as a speechwriter for Ronald Reagan and both Bush Administrations, is a senior fellow at the Ethics and Public Policy Center, a conservative think tank, and a fellow at the Trinity Forum, a nonprofit Christian organization, would write that these factions were "attracted to racial and ethnic politics and moved by resentment and intolerance, rather than a vision of the good." At critical moments, "the Republican Party either overlooked them or played to them." Some may have tried appealing to these elements in hopes of containing and moderating them, "to sand off the rough edges, to keep them within the coalition but not allow them to become dominant. But the opposite happened."[140]

Wehner's observations and counsel seem to have channeled an extension of those Raggio made years earlier. Raggio had also realized that Reagan's "Big Tent," of which he had been so proud in welcoming everyone into the Republican Party, had become a hodgepodge of radical political ideologies. These extremists, he said, would quietly take over the party apparatus, from local precinct, through the state to the national level, catching traditional Republicans by surprise. Wehner summed it up more succinctly: "The guests took over the party."

Conservative journalist David Brooks wrote that these "guests:"

> Live in a state of perpetual war; they need to continually invent existential foes—critical race theory, nongendered bathrooms, out-of-control immigration. They need to treat half the country, metropolitan America, as a moral cancer and view the cultural and demographic changes of the past fifty years as an alien invasion.

Raggio had also been offended, not just by the ultraconservatives' assault on decorum and civility but by their absence of factual representation, reason, and accountability. Building his trial cases based upon constitutionally ensured rules of evidence had made Raggio famous as a prosecutor, successfully guiding juries through the labyrinth of prevarications and logical fallacies defense attorneys often employed in their efforts to establish reasonable doubt. These were the rules he played by, and so was affronted by those who based their decisions on self-serving falsehoods and unprovable conspiracy theories. He knew that, ultimately, politics and society break down when there is no common ground.

Throughout his life, Raggio marveled at the genius of the Founders, who devised the Constitution–through relentless debate and negotiation–that, if obeyed, would provide its citizens with rights and protections unheard of in that age of tyranny.

Against his party's increasingly anti-government tone, Raggio often invoked the Preamble, which described the purpose of government and the duty of legislators to guarantee justice, ensure domestic tranquility, provide for the common defense, promote the general welfare, and keep liberty secure for current and future generations of Americans. Despite this being the basis for the highest law in the land, it was no longer the ethos or message of his long-cherished GOP.

In 2011, several months before his death, Raggio prophetically expressed his defiance: "We have a Republican Party that seems intent on eating its own, and it is going to have serious political consequences."

The End

SOURCES

INTERVIEWS

Brezny, Joe (Carson City) April 22, 2009

Brower, Greg (Las Vegas) October 18, 2021

Bryan, Richard (Reno) August 21, 2008

Buckley, Barbara (Las Vegas) April 2, 2010

Cashell, Bob (Reno) February 2, 2010

Clift, Claire Jesse (Carson City) April 2, 2021

Dickens, Robert (Reno) June 9, 2008

Ferraro, Greg (Reno) March 10, 2011

Goodman, Oscar (Las Vegas) February 27, 2009

Guinn, Kenny (Reno) September 8, 2009

Hansen, Ira (Carson City) November 24, 2021

Hardy, Joe (Boulder City), November 1, 2021

Hardy II, Warren (Las Vegas) November 18, 2021

Hickey, Pat (Reno) April 5, 2022

James, Mark (Las Vegas) October 25, 2009

Kieckhefer, Ben (Reno) December 1, 2021

Laxalt, Paul (Washington, D.C.) June 10, 2008

Malkiewich, Lorne (Carson City) March 27, 2008

Myers, Dennis (Sparks) July 17, 2008

Raggio, Dale (Carson City) March 18, 2009

Raggio, William J., by Tom King (5 separate interviews) January 20, 21 & 24, 1999, and October 19, 1999

Raggio, William J., (18 separate interviews) February 4, 2008—May 13, 2010

Reid, Harry (Washington, D.C.) August 20, 2010 and August 10, 2021

Rose, Bob (Reno) November 7, 2010

Scheberle, Ron (Dallas) June 11, 2009/December 1, 2022

Titus, Dina (Washington, D.C.) March 4, 2010

Townsend, Randolph (Reno) January 7, 2010, April 19, 2022 and March 15, 2023

Watson, Jerry (Carson City) March 14, 2009

Wynn, Steve (Las Vegas) March 27, 2010

SELECT BIBLIOGRAPHY

Archer, Michael, *A Man of His Word, The Life & Times of Nevada's Senator William J, Raggio*, Hellgate Press, 2011.

Bayley, Edwin R., *Joe McCarthy and the Press*, University of Wisconsin Press, 1981.

Bennett, William J., *America: The Last Best Hope*, Thomas Nelson, 2019.

Boehner, John, *On the House: A Washington Memoir*, New York: St. Martin's Press, 2021.

Bowers, Michael W., *The Sagebrush State, Nevada's History, Government and Politics*, Reno: University of Nevada Press, 2002.

Cegavske, Barbara, *Political History of Nevada (12th Edition)*, Carson City: State Printing Office, 2016.

Dickens, Robert E., *The Maverick Spirit: Building the New Nevada— William Raggio: Personality, Power, and Politics,* edited by Richard O. Davies, Reno: University of Nevada Press, 1999.

Driggs, Don W. and Leonard E. Goodall, *Nevada Politics & Government: Conservatism in an Open Society*, Lincoln: University of Nebraska Press, 1996.

Elliott, Russell R., *History of Nevada*, University of Nebraska Press, 1987.

Hamill, Pete, *Why Sinatra Matters*, New York, Little, Brown & Company, 1998.

Harman, Chris, *The Fire Last Time: 1968 and After*, London and Chicago, Bookmarks. 1998.

Heller, Dean, *Political History of Nevada (11th Edition)*, Carson City: State Printing Office, 2006.

Kutler, Stanley I., *Abuse of Power: The New Nixon Tapes*, New York, Touchstone, 1998.

Laxalt, Paul, *Nevada's Paul Laxalt, A Memoir*, Reno: Jack Bacon & Company, 2000.

Laxalt, Robert, *Nevada, A History*, Reno: University of Nevada Press, 1977.

Mann, Thomas E. & Ornstein, Norman J., *It's Even Worse Than It Looks: How the American Constitutional System Collided with the New Politics of Extremism*, Basic Books, 2012.

Marvel, John W., interviewed by Dana R. Bennett, Nevada Legislature Oral History Project, December 1, 2008.

Neal, Joe M. Jr., interviewed by Dana R. Bennett, Nevada Legislature Oral History Project, May 12, 2008.

O'Connell, Ann, interviewed by Dana R. Bennett and Dale A.R. Erquiaga, Nevada Legislature Oral History Project, March 28, 2008.

Ralston, Jon, *The Anointed One*, Las Vegas, Huntington Press, 2000.

Rawson, Raymond E., interviewed by Dana R. Bennett, Nevada Legislature Oral History Project, May 12, 2008.

Sawyer, Grant, Gary Elliott, and R.T. King, *Hang Tough*! Reno: University of Nevada Oral History Program, 1993.

Smith, John L., *Of Rats and Men: Oscar Goodman's Life from Mob Mouthpiece to Mayor of Las Vegas*, Las Vegas: Huntington Press, 2003.

Summers, Anthony, *Official and Confidential: The Secret Life of J. Edgar Hoover*, G. P. Putnam, 1993.

Wagner, Sue and Victoria Ford, *Through the Glass Ceiling*, Reno: University of Nevada
Oral History Program, 2005.

Welch, Robert E., *The Blue Book of the John Birch Society*, American Opinion Books, 1962.

ABOUT THE AUTHOR

MICHAEL ARCHER is the author of several books including, *A Man of His Word: The Life & Times of Nevada's Senator William J. Raggio; A Patch of Ground: Khe Sanh Remembered; The Long Goodbye: Khe Sanh Revisited; and The Gunpowder Prince: How Marine Corps Captain Mirza Munir Baig Saved Khe Sanh.*

In addition, Michael's articles and essays have appeared the *Nevada Review, Political History of Nevada—2016,* and *Naval History* magazine.

His work has been honored by Foreword Magazine's INDIES Book of the Year Award and received literary awards from the Marine Corps Heritage Foundation in the categories of distinguished biography and feature writing.

Michael served in the United States Marine Corps, studied history at California State University, Sacramento and worked in both federal and state government, including nine legislative sessions as a staff member with the Nevada State Senate.

Michael is regularly invited to speak to organizations, colleges and universities across the country. A native of Oakland, California, he has resided in Northern Nevada since 1978.

CHAPTER NOTES

[1] Jude Wanniski, *"Dick Tracy, Sam Spade Equals Reno's Mr. Raggio,"* *Las Vegas Review Journal*, 29 April, 1965. (Reprinted with permission from the then-editor of the *Las Vegas Review Journal*.).

[2] Don W. Driggs and Leonard E. Goodall, *Nevada Politics and Government: Conservatism in an Open Society*, (*University* of Nebraska Press 1996),76.

[3] Dickens, Robert E., *"William Raggio: Personality, Power, and Politics,"* The Maverick Spirit: Building the New Nevada, edited by Richard O. Davies (Reno: University of Nevada Press, 1999), 226-227. .

[4] The 1960 census showed Nevada's population as being 285,278, ranging from as many as 127,016 people in Clark County to as few as 568 in Storey County. With seventeen members in the state Senate, apportioned one per county, the ratio of representation between Clark and Story Counties was astonishingly imbalanced at 224 to 1.

[5] In 1962, the U.S. Supreme Court ruled in *Baker vs. Carr* that federal courts could act in cases in which action, or inaction, by state legislatures led to malapportionment. This was followed in 1964, by *Reynolds v. Sims*, in which the high court interpreted the federal constitution to require that both houses of state legislatures be apportioned on the basis of population, referred to then as the "one-man-one-vote rule."

[6] *Roe v. Wade* held that a mother may abort her pregnancy, for any reason, during the first six months. The Court based its ruling on the mother's constitutional right to privacy provided in the Due Process Clause of the Fourteenth Amendment. At the time of this decision, abortion was legal in only four states: Alaska, Hawaii, Washington and New York. In Nevada, abortion was illegal, except to save the life of the mother or another child.

[7] Also, in 1990, Republican Senator Sue Wagner would make a bold political move of another kind. Sensing conservative legislators would attempt to change the state's eighteen-year-old law permitting abortion, Wagner led a drive for a referendum to have the public enact a statute bringing the state into compliance with *Roe v. Wade*. Question 7 won handily and prohibited the Legislature from changing Nevada's abortion law without a new referendum.

Outside observers might find such overwhelming support for this measure at odds with the conservative bent of Nevadans, especially considering their recent rejection of the ERA. However, as political scientists Driggs and Goodall pointed out, Nevada's individualistic political culture "focuses on the centrality of private concerns."

This culture, they suggested, placed a premium on limiting both governmental and non-governmental community intervention into private activities to keep the marketplace. Viewed from outside Nevada, this attitude was most apparent in the legalization of prostitution in much of Nevada.

"The 'right of privacy,'" they added, "was also important to the typical Nevadan, as evidenced by 63 percent of the electorate voting in 1990 to restrict the Legislature from making changes in the 1973 abortion law."

[8] "Democrats Add 44 In House, 4 In Senate!" *Desert Sun,*" November 6, 1974.

[9] *Reno Evening Gazette*, October 27, 1976.

[10] Edwin R. Bayley, *Joe McCarthy and the Press* (University of Wisconsin Press, 1981), 51.

[11] "Eisenhower Remarks at Fourth Annual Republican Women's National Conference," *The American Presidency Project,* University of California, Santa Barbara, accessed October 1, 2021. https://www.presidency.ucsb.edu/documents/remarks-fourth-annual-republican-women-s-national-conference

[12] Ronald Kessler, "Joe McCarthy: Dangerous Buffoon,*" History News Network,*. https://historynewsnetwork.org/article/1568

[13] Edward R. Murrow, CBS-TV "A Report on Senator Joseph R. McCarthy," March 9, 1954, https://www.cbsnews.com/news/edward-r-murrow-joseph-mccarthy-report-1954/

[14] Senator Joseph R. McCarthy, "Reply to Edward R. Murrow," *See It Now*" CBS-TV. April 6, 1954, https://www.billdownscbs.com/2015/10/1954-senator-joseph-mccarthy-responds.html

[15] Robert E. Welch, *The Blue Book of the John Birch Society*, American Opinion Books, 1962.

[16] Sean Wilentz, "Cofounding Fathers," *New Yorker*, October 18, 2010, https://www.newyorker.com/magazine/2010/10/18/confounding-fathers

[17] Richard K. Rovere, "The Campaign: Goldwater" *New Yorker*, 2021.https://www.newyorker.com/magazine/1964/10/03/the-campaign-goldwater

18 "Goldwater's 1964 Acceptance Speech", Washington Post (archives), https://www.washingtonpost.com/wp-srv/politics/daily/may98/goldwaterspeech.htm

19 Dickens, *"Personality, Power, and Politics," 225.*

20 Nick Koz, *Judgement Days: Lyndon Baines Johnson, Martin Luther King, Jr., and the Laws That Changed America*, (New York, Houghton Mifflin), 2005.

21"Civil Rights in America: Racial Voting Rights," *National Historic Landmarks Program Cultural Resources, National Park Service, U.S. Department of the Interior*, 2009, accessed December 2, 2021 https://www.nps.gov/subjects/tellingallamericansstories/upload/CivilRights_VotingRights.pdf, 2009, 35.

22 It was not until 1913, after the 17th amendment to the Constitution was passed, the Senators were elected a popular vote. Prior to this they were chosen by state legislatures. Part of the haggling over the amendment was a fear in the Deep South that Blacks would be able to vote, and so unsuccessfully demanded a "race rider." From this point on, the federal government could insinuate itself into state elections where federal level candidates are running, https://www.archives.gov/milestone-documents/17th-amendment.

23 George Breitman, *By Any Means Necessary: Speeches, Interviews, and a Letter by Malcolm X.*, (New York: Pathfinder Press), 1970.

24 Virginia Postrel, "The Consequences of the 1960's Race Riots Come into View," *New York Times*, December 30, 2004, https://www.nytimes.com/2004/12/30/business/the-consequences-of-the-1960s-race-riots-come-into-view.html

[25]David Paul Kuhn, "The Day the White Working Class Turned Republican," *New York Times* July 1, 2020, https://www.nytimes.com/2020/07/01/books/review/the-hardhat-riot-david-paul-kuhn.html

[26] "Students for a Democratic Society (SDS)," *Influence Watch,* accessed January 6, 2022, https://www.influencewatch.org/non-profit/students-for-a-democratic-society-sds/

[27] Chris Harman, *The Fire Last Time: 1968 and After* (London and Chicago: Bookmarks: 1998), 176.

[28] "The Sixties," Internet Archive Wayback Machine, accessed November 14, 2021. https://web.archive.org/web/20060328145901/http://martinrealm.org/documents/radical/sixties1.html

[29] Ronald Reagan speech "The Time for Choosing" October 27, 1964, https://www.reaganlibrary.gov/reagans/ronald-reagan/time-choosing-speech-october-27-1964

[30] *The Atlantic,* https://www.theatlantic.com/magazine/archive/2018/11/newt-gingrich-says-youre-welcome/570832/

[31] Steven Levitsky and Daniel Ziblatt, "How a Democracy Dies" *The New Republic,* December 11, 2018.

[32]Ibid.

[33] Thomas Mann & Norma Ornstein, *It's Even Worse Than It Looks:*

How the American Constitutional System Collided with the New Politics of Extremism.

[34] Nicholas Valentino, David Sears, "Old Times There Are Not Forgotten: Race and Partisan Realignment in the Contemporary South, *American Journal of Political Science*, July 2005,49.

[35] Juli Weiner, "Ron Paul Watch, With Ron Paul, Presidential Candidate: Day Seven," *Vanity Fair,* September 7, 2011. https://www.vanityfair.com/news/2011/09/ron-paul-watch--with-ron-paul--presidential-candidate--day-seven

[36] S.A. Paolanonio, "Libertarian Seeks Presidency Third Party Tries a 5th Campaign". *Philadelphia Inquirer,* September 13, 1987.

[37]Dennis Myers, "Evolution: Republican Bill Raggio Went from Militancy to Moderation. The GOP Went the Other Way." *Reno News & Review*, January11, 2011.

[38] Dickens, "Personality, Power, and Politics," p.226.

[39] *Reno Gazette-Journal*, 18 January 1989.

[40] *Las Vegas Review-Journal*, 18 October 1990.

[41] *Las Vegas Review-Journal*, 7 July 1991.

[42] *Reno Gazette-Journal*, 30 June 1991.

[43] Jon Ralston, *Reno Gazette-Journal*, April 15, 1996.

[44] Randall E. King, "When Worlds Collide: Politics, Religion, and Media at the 1970 East Tennessee Billy Graham Crusade. (Appearance by President Richard M. Nixon)," *Journal of Church and State*, May 17, 2011.

Daniel K. Williams, "Jerry Falwell's Sunbelt Politics: The Regional Origins of the Moral Majority," *Journal of Policy History* (Cambridge University Press), April 2010.

[45] Jimmy Carter, *White House Diary,* 2010 New York, N.Y: Farrar, Straus and Giroux, 2010. 469.

[46] "Falwell Speaks About WTC Disaster," *Christian Broadcasting Network*," October 19, 2012.

[47] Ryan Burge, "Are We All Evangelicals Now? How The Term Has Grown to Blur Theology and Ideology," Religion Unplugged, accessed January 6, 2022. https://religionunplugged.com/news/2021/3/11/are-we-all-evangelicals-now-how-the-term-has-grown-to-blur-theology-and-ideology?rq=evangelical&gclid=Cj0KCQjww4OMBhCUARIsAILndv4vW VlcORp2SDpgZxrcF3

[48] Andrew Whitehead, Samuel L.; Perry, *Taking America Back for God: Christian Nationalism in the United States*, (Oxford University Press, 2020),

[49] Gospel of Matthew 12:30, https://biblehub.com/matthew/12-30.htm.

[50] "Pastors Fret Christian Group Might be a Threat," *StarNewsOnline.com.*, December 14, 2021. https://culteducation.com/group/870-christian-exodus/3680-pastors-fret-christian-group-might-be-a-threat.html

---

[51] *Religion and the Presidential Vote,* Pew Research Center for the People and the Press, December 6, 2004.

[52] Neal Gabler, *Winchell: Gossip, Power, and the Culture of Celebrity,* (Knopf, 1994) 8-9.

[53] Carl Sagan, *Demon-Haunted World: Science as a Candle in the Dark*, (Ballantine Books, 1996), 25.

[54] Colin Crouch, *Post-Democracy*, (Polity, 2004).

[55] Sagan, op. cit.

[56] Grant Sawyer, Gary Elliott, R.T. King, *Hang Tough*! (Reno, University of Nevada Oral History Program,1993), 91.

[57] "Raggio says O'Donnell's Quitting Won't Hurt Nevada's Republicans," *Las Vegas Sun,* August 13, 2001. https://lasvegassun.com/news/2001/aug/13/raggio-says-odonnells-quitting-wont-hurt-nevadas-r/.

[58] Myers, *Evolution*, op. cit.

[59] Townsend, op. cit., April 21, 2022. Regarding term limits, Townsend recalled that "in Nevada, a voter initiative petition brought this to a head, and at that time, the law would have required term limits to apply to both judges and legislators. The judges immediately took it to the Supreme Court, and it was ruled that, because of the separation of powers, the initiative petition would not apply to them, and so they were excluded. If the Legislature had done that and gotten the same ruling, term limits likely would have failed. But they decided to wait until the first legislator was termed out to challenge the validity of the law, and it was too late."

⁶⁰ David McGrath Schwartz, "Nevada's Tax Income from Gaming Well Below Other Markets," *Las Vegas Sun,* October 7, 2011. https://lasvegassun.com/news/2011/oct/07/nevadas-tax-income-gaming-well-below-other-markets/

⁶¹"Quotes on Governor Kenny Guinn's State of the State Address," *Las Vegas Sun*, January 21, 2003. https://lasvegassun.com/news/2003/jan/21/quotes-on-gov-kenny-guinns-state-of-the-state-addr/

⁶² "Taxpayer Protection Pledge" *Americans for Tax Reform,* accessed November 14, 2021. https://web.archive.org/web/20111215134121/http://www.atr.org/userfiles/StatePledge.pdf

⁶³ Chuck Muth, "Tax Pledge Signers Not Irrelevant We Just Need More of Them," June 9, 2011, https://www.nevadaappeal.com/news/opinion/chuck-muth-tax-pledge-signers-not-irrelevant-we-just-need-more-of-them/

⁶⁴ Ibid.

⁶⁵ Bowers, *Sagebrush*, op. cit.

⁶⁶ Ibid.

⁶⁷ Per Townsend, Rawson was voted out because he was considered too liberal despite being a traditionally conservative member of the Latter-Day Saints. Businesses worried that he might agree to raise taxes. O'Connell, on the other hand lost to powerful

gaming interests because she refused to consider a business tax.

⁶⁸ *Reno Gazette Journal*, 23 January 2007.

⁶⁹ Jennifer Steinhauer, "Nevada Challenger Lifted by Tea Party Ardor," *New York Times*, June 9, 2010. https://www.nytimes.com/2010/06/10/us/politics/10nevada.

⁷⁰ "Gibbons Names New Press Secretary," *Las Vegas Review-Journal*, November 11, 2008. https://www.reviewjournal.com/news/gibbons-names-new-press-secretary/

⁷¹ Notable Nevadans who did sign include Governor Jim Gibbons, Lieutenant Governor Brian Krolicki, Congressman Dean Heller, U.S. Senator John Ensign, State Senator Barbara Cegavske and Assemblywoman Sharron Angle.

⁷³ Molly Ball, "Assembly Passes Tax Bill," *Las Vegas Review,* May 22, 2009, https://www.reviewjournal.com/uncategorized/assembly-passes-tax-bill/

⁷⁴ Jon Ralston, Las *Vegas Sun*, May 24, 2009.

⁷⁵ Jon Ralston, *RalstonFlash,* February 28, 2010, RalstonFlash-ralston@vegas.com

⁷⁶ David McGrath Schwartz, "Governor Seems to Be Backsliding on Pledge Not to Raise Taxes," Las *Vegas Sun*, February 13, 2010.

⁷⁷ Raggio was also concerned that the first session to be impacted by

a large influx of new faces in the Legislature due to term limits would be 2011, a session that would require reapportionment and redistricting. Because Nevada had experienced such rapid growth over the last decade, it was probable that a fourth seat in the House of Representatives would be added. The Legislature would also have to decide whether to expand in size beyond its current sixty-three members. In July, the issue became moot when the Supreme Court unanimously upheld term limits and clarified what constituted a "twelve-year term."

[78] David M. Drucker and Anna Palmer, "Reid Leads Fundraising Drive," *Roll Call*, September 22, 2010. https://rollcall.com/2010/09/22/reid-leads-fundraising-drive/.

[79] The Tea Party political movement was a loose affiliation of national and local groups representing varying platforms and agendas and staging protests around the country. Its most common theme was opposition to government taxation and spending policies, the name derived from the Boston Tea Party of 1773. Its base was composed primarily of white working-class voters who labeled themselves as the great conservative majority and who felt overwhelming resentment toward what they perceived to be a government unresponsive to their needs and a Republican Party led by elites and "establishment" politicians who were unwilling to change things.

[80] Richard Kim, "Roots of the Tea Party Conspiracy Mania," *The Nation,* March 26, 2010.

[81] Michael Mishack, Sharron Angle Wins; Harry Reid Gets the Race He Wanted, *"Las Vegas Sun,* June 9, *2010.* https://lasvegassun.com/news/2010/jun/09/angles-win-has-reids-touch/

[82] Laura Myers, "Political Eye: GOP Senate Race Reflects Gotcha Game," *Las Vegas Review-Journal,* May 24, 2010.

[83] Sam Stein, "Angle Thinks It's Wrong for Both Parents to Hold Jobs Simultaneously," *Huffington Post*. June 9, 2010.

[84] Evan Lehmann, ""Reid, in Fistfight, Could Take More Punches from Climate Bill," *New York Times*, May 26, 2010.

[85] Anjeanette Damon, "Armed Revolt Part of Sharron Angle's Rhetoric," *Las Vegas Sun,* June 17, 2010.

[86] Steve Tetreault, "Another Angle Issue Emerges," *Las Vegas Review-Journal*, June 15, 2010.

[87] Jon Ralston, "Harry Reid Was More Complicated Than You Knew," *Politico, December 29, 2021.* https://www.politico.com/news/magazine/2021/12/29/harry-reid-nevada-526244?utm_source=facebook&utm_medium=news_tab

[88] Ray Hagar, "Rogich: Reid 'probably' Nevada's Most Important Elected Official," *Nevada Appeal*, December 30, 2021. https://www.nevadaappeal.com/news/2021/dec/30/rogich-reid-probably-nevadas-most-important-electe/

[89] Ferraro, op. cit.

[90] Laura Myers, "Angle Dismisses Raggio as 'good ol' boy career Politician' After he Endorses Reid," *Las Vegas Review-Journal*, October 7, 2010.

[91] Michael Shear, "Ryan Brings the Tea Party to the Ticket," *New York Times,* August 12, 2012.

[92] Muth, op. cit.

[93] Brower, op. cit.

[94] *Reno Gazette Journal*, 6 January 2011.

[95] O'Connell, Oral History, op. cit.

[96] Jon Ralston, *Las Vegas Sun*, January 7, 2011.

[97] "Angle Says Raggio's Departure No Surprise," *This is Reno,* accessed December 20, 2021. https://thisisreno.com/2011/01/angle-says-raggio-departure-no-surprise/

[98] Jerry Watson interview with Michael Archer, 14 March 2009.

[99] Scheberle interview, December 1, 2022.

[100] Author's personal recollection while in attendance.

[101] Scheberle interviewer, 1 December 2022. Scheberle added that by 2014, twelve out of the twenty-one major corporations had pulled out of ALEC in an effort to distance themselves ultra-right policies being put forward by the organization. By the end of the decade, ALEC had lost all but its most extreme members and was spearheading election fraud charges and other conspiracies theories.

[102] Jerry Gray, "Kemp Hits Back at Republicans Who Despair," *New York Times*, October 26, 1996.

[103] Eddings, Jerelyn; Jeannye Thornton; Dorian Friedman; Josh Chetwynd; Kevin Whitelaw; Victoria Pope, "Voices from the Gallery: Fearful and Eager, Voters Are Talking Up a Storm of Worries and Wishes". *U.S. News & World Report*. Archived from the original on May 24, 2011. Retrieved April 14, 2008.

[104] *The Atlantic,*

https://www.theatlantic.com/politics/archive/2015/10/jack-kemp-legacy/410152/

[105] David F. Damore, "Latinos Rising: Consequences of the 2011 Nevada Redistricting," *Latino Decisions* (University of Nevada, Las Vegas), December 26, 2011.

[106] Jon Ralston, *Las Vegas Sun*, November 6, 2011.

[107] "Appeal Reporter Remembers Raggio as a Man for All the People," *Nevada Appeal*, February 25, 2012. https://www.nevadaappeal.com/news/2012/feb/25/appeal-reporter-remembers-raggio-as-a-man-for-all-/

[108] Ralston, "Harry Reid Was More Complicated," op. cit.

[109] Kevin Cirilli, "Paul: Secession 'deeply American,'" *Politico,* November 19, 2012. https://www.politico.com/story/2012/11/paul-secession-deeply-american-084058

[110] In the Nevada, Assembly speakers are elected by an open vote, rather than an intra-majority party vote.

[111] Dennis Myers, "On Paper, Republican Leader Left a Trail," *Reno News & Review,* November 20, 2014. https://www.newsreview.com/reno/content/on-paper/15531962/

[112] Michael A. Memoli, "Eric Cantor Upset: How Dave Brat Pulled Off a Historic Political Coup," Los Angeles Times, June 11, 2014: https://www.latimes.com/nation/politics/politicsnow/la-pn-eric-cantor-dave-brat-primary-20140611-story.html

[113] Sabrina Eaton, "House Republican Leader John Boehner of Ohio Helps Unite GOP," *Cleveland Plain Dealer,* March 8, 2009.

[114] John Boehner, *On the House: A Washington Memoir,* New York: St. Martin's Press, 2021.

[115] Boehner. op.cit.

[116] Thomas E. Mann, Norman J. Ornstein, *It's Even Worse Than It Looks: How the American Constitutional System Collided with the New Politics of Extremism,"* Basic Books, 2012.

[117] Maggie Haberbam, "RNC: Voters See GOP as 'Scary'," *Politico,* March 18, 2013. https://www.politico.com/story/2013/03/rnc-report-gop-scary-out-of-touch-088974

[118] David Folkenflik, "You Literally Can't Believe the Facts Tucker Carlson Tells You. So Say Fox's Lawyers," *NPR*, September 29, 2020. https://www.npr.org/2020/09/29/917747123/you-literally-cant-believe-the-facts-tucker-carlson-tells-you-so-say-fox-s-lawye

[119] Michael Moore "Five Reasons Why Trump Will Win," accessed January 6, 2022, https://michaelmoore.com/trumpwillwin/

[120] David Brooks, "What Happened to American Conservatism?" *Atlantic,* January/February 2022. https://www.theatlantic.com/magazine/archive/2022/01/brooks-true-conservatism-dead-fox-news-voter-suppression/620853/?utm_source=facebook&utm_medium=cr&utm_campaign=WITHIN_Prospecting_Content_BidCap&utm_term=WITHIN_LaLSubscribers_082521&utm_content=010422_DR_Image_WhatHappened_Americ

anConservatism_ContentLP_LearnMore%20-
%20Copy&fbclid=IwAR361mqwsT5OEcgh-
_AVOejXAVTRVzo91Ko1UwAozYCwGtriP9MajppH2sI

[121] Julian E. Zelizer, "How Newt Gingrich Played the Groundwork
for Trump's Republican Party," *TIME,* July 7, 2020.
https://time.com/5863457/how-newt-gingrich-laid-the-groundwork-
for-trumps-republican-party/

[122] Nevada Office of Secretary of State, Elections, accessed January
4, 2022. https://www.nvsos.gov/sos/elections/voters/voter-registration-
statistics

[123] Scott Sonner (AP). "Tech Boom, Suburban Growth Drive
Nevada's Democratic Shift," *ABC News*, February 20, 2020.
https://abcnews.go.com/Politics/wireStory/tech-boom-suburban-growth-
drive-nevadas-democratic-shift-69118279

[124] Sonner, "Tech Boom, op. cit.

[125] Drew Desilver, "Turnout soared in 2020 as nearly two-thirds of
eligible U.S. voters cast ballots for president," *Pew Center*, January 28, 2021.
https://www.pewresearch.org/fact-tank/2021/01/28/turnout-soared-in-2020-
as-nearly-two-thirds-of-eligible-u-s-voters-cast-ballots-for-president/

[126] Martin Tolchin, "G.O.P. Memo Tells of Black Vote Cut, *New
York Times,* October 25, 1986.
https://www.nytimes.com/1986/10/25/us/gop-memo-tells-of-black-vote-
cut.html

[127] "Select Committee to Investigate the January 6 Attack on the
United States Capitol," 117th Congress Second Session, House Report 117-

000, December 00, 2022. https://www.cnn.com/2022/12/22/politics/full-jan-6-report/index.html.

[128] Elliott Hannon, "Poll Finds Nearly 40 Percent of Republicans Think Political Violence Is Justifiable and Could Be Necessary," *Slate*, February 11, 2021 https://slate.com/news-and-politics/2021/02/aei-poll-40-percent-republicans-conservatives-political-violence.html.

[129] Chris Cillizza, "Why Mitch McConnell's Comment About the January 6 Committee Matters," *CNN Politics*, December 16, 2021. https://www.cnn.com/2021/12/15/politics/mitch-mcconnell-january-6/index.html

[130] Boehner, *On the House*, op. cit., 190.

[131] James R. Skillen, "Justice — Beginning with Cliven Bundy," *Nevada Independent,* January 24, 2021. https://thenevadaindependent.com/article/justice-beginning-with-cliven-bundy

[132] "Editorial: "New Vote Not Warranted," *Las Vegas Review Journal*, August 29 2006.

[133] Jennifer Epstein, "Sharron's Angle: Harry Stole Election," *Politico*, June 10, 2011, https://www.politico.com/story/2011/06/sharrons-angle-harry-stole-election-056698.

[134] Michelle Rindels, "Departing Secretary of State Cegavske: 'I just stuck up for the law'" *Nevada Independent,* December 23, 2022. https://thenevadaindependent.com/article/departing-secretary-of-state-cegavske-i-just-stuck-up-for-the-law.

135 Riley Snyder, "Nevada Republicans Vote to Censure SOS Cegavske Over Voter Fraud Allegations," *Nevada Independent*, April 10, 2021. https://thenevadaindependent.com/article/nevada-republicans-vote-to-censure-sos-cegavske-over-voter-fraud-allegations

136 Steve Sebelius, "Voter Fraud in the 2022 Election?" *Las Vegas Review-Journal,* December 3, 2022. https://www.reviewjournal.com/opinion/opinion-columns/steve-sebelius/steve-sebelius-voter-fraud-in-the-2022-election-2687602/?fbclid=IwAR0j9_wJ9qXU-XWPk8pGmFWgPCnu8U3jXtPH1zPey_QGhTMgY0rWwD_73d8

137 Jeff Greenfield, "Kevin McCarthy Is a Victim of Republican Ingenuity," *Politico,* January 4, 2023. https://www.politico.com/news/magazine/2023/01/04/kevin-mccarthy-gop-vote-00076263.

138 In twenty-two U.S. states, at least one political party conducts open primaries for congressional and state-level officials. Sixteen states have open primaries for presidential primaries and caucuses.

139 Rick Perlstein, "I Thought I Understood the American Right. Trump Proved Me Wrong: A historian of conservatism looks back at how he and his peers failed to anticipate the rise of the president," *New York Times*, April 11, 2017 https://www.nytimes.com/2017/04/11/magazine/i-thought-i-understood-the-american-right-trump-proved-me-wrong.html

140 "What Will Trump's Legacy Be After Leaving Office?" *PBS Newshour*, January 19, 2019. https://www.pbs.org/newshour/show/what-will-trumps-legacy-be-after-leaving-office